THE FAMILY DISCIPLESHIP HANDBOOK

DR. JERRY MACGREGOR

Christian Parenting
BOOKS

ACKNOWLEDGEMENTS
I would like to thank the Bevers, Andersons and Rogers, Godparents
of our children, for getting it right. My grateful appreciation to Gary
Wilde for his dynamite job of editing my manuscript, and to Dave Horton
of Chariot Family Publishing for believing in this project.

Unless otherwise specified, Scripture quotations are from the *Holy Bible:
New International Version* ©1973, 1978, 1984 by International Bible
Society. Used by permission of Zondervan Bible Publishers.

Christian Parenting Books is an imprint of Chariot Family Publishing,
a div. of David C. Cook Publishing Co.
David C. Cook Publishing Co., Elgin, Illinois 60120
David C. Cook Publishing Co., Weston, Ontario
Nova Distribution Ltd., Newton Abbot, England

THE FAMILY DISCIPLESHIP HANDBOOK
©1993 by Jerry MacGregor

Cover design by Foster Design Associates
Interior Design by Glass House Graphics
Edited by Gary Wilde

First Printing, 1993
Printed in the United States of America
97 96 95 94 93 5 4 3 2 1

CIP Applied for.
ISBN 0-78140-837-7

This book is dedicated to my wife, Patti,
the best mom I know.

THE FAMILY DISCIPLESHIP HANDBOOK

❦

"I just wish someone would show me how to disciple my kids."

It was raining again in Portland. Dave Anderson sat in church and stared out the side window, watching the drops slithering down the pale yellow glass. The pastor was wrapping up his message on Deuteronomy 6.

"These are the commands, decrees and laws the LORD your God directed me to teach you to observe . . . . so that you, your children and their children after them may fear the LORD your God as long as you live by keeping all his decrees and commands that I give you, and so that you may enjoy long life."

Okay, I believe that, Dave said to himself as he focused again on the pastor. *We've got to know the Scriptures so we can obey them.*

"Hear, O Israel: The LORD our God, the Lord is one. Love the Lord your God with all your heart and with all your soul and with all your strength."

Right, thought Dave. *But that isn't the problem. I already love God.*

"These commandments that I give you today are to be upon your hearts."

5

Uh-oh. Here it comes.

> "Impress them on your children. Talk about them when you sit at home and when you walk along the road, when you lie down and when you get up. Tie them as symbols on your hands and bind them on your foreheads. Write them on the doorframes of your houses and on your gates."

Dave thought of all the times he had tried talking to his kids about the Bible. He pictured sitting around the living room, the kids squirming as he read the Bible verses, fighting during prayers, sitting sullenly during the hymn, then making a dash for it when Dad said, "Well, I guess that's enough."

I've heard these verses a thousand times! Dave felt like standing up in church and asking, "Excuse me, but could you just show me *how* to do it? I'm not creative; I can never find the time in my crazy schedule, and I don't need to be convinced that what the Scripture says is right. I know it's right. I just don't know how to do it!" But, of course, he didn't stand and say anything. He just sat through the closing illustration and final hymn, grabbed his Bible and umbrella, and made for the car.

"That's it, Kim, I mean it," he said to his wife. "No more."

Kim, who had had this conversation with her husband before, waited him out.

"I know the girls need more from me; I know I'm supposed to be teaching them, but I can't do it. Maybe I don't have what it takes, but . . ." he waited, not sure how to phrase his reasons. "Man, I'm so tired of feeling like a failure as a spiritual leader. I'm sick to death of being told what to do without being told *how* to do it. I just wish someone would show me how to disciple my kids."

Kim thought the time was right. "I have an idea," she offered.

A sigh. "Okay. Let's hear it."

"Let's talk with the Bevers."

"Who?"

"You know. They're the new couple who moved into the yellow house on Brookwood Street. I've been talking with the wife, and she seems to have a lot of good ideas about teaching the Bible to her kids."

"Where do they go to church?"

"First Church," Kim replied, referring to a large neighborhood congregation. "Bob is a businessman of some kind, and he really seems to know children. Last Saturday when I took the girls for a walk we stopped in to say 'Hi' and their family was in the middle of some sort of game. The children were trying to mimic what their dad was doing, but they were also talking about how we are to imitate Christ. Bob invited the girls to join in the game and they loved it. Later they traced some patterns and colored some pictures."

"So?"

"Well, in the midst of playing games the kids got a great lesson in following Jesus. I asked Susan about it and she said that's how they have devotions."

"Doesn't sound like devotions to me."

"Yes, I know, but it accomplished the same thing."

They drove on in silence for awhile, then Kim added: "Let's stop by the Bevers. I'll call Susan and ask if we could drop by on Saturday."

After a pause, Dave replied, "Okay. Can't hurt, I guess."

❦

"We keep it a secret. . . .We don't let them know they're having devotions!"

The Andersons weren't the only visitors that Saturday. Bob Bever's parents had arrived to help the couple get settled in

7

their new home, and the grandparents were regaling the kids with stories about all the crazy things their dad had done when he was a youngster. The Bevers' three children, Sarah, Emily, and Daniel, were sitting on the couch with their grandparents, and they had invited the Anderson's three girls to join them. During dinner they had read Ephesians 5:22-25, discussing together what it means to love someone "as Christ loved the church." After the meal Bob and Susan Bever had quizzed the kids on their parents' marriage, asking questions like: "Where did we go on our first date?" "When did Dad ask me to marry him?" and "How long will I love your mother?" Now, with the kids in the family room giggling at Grandpa's tall tales, Dave and Kim sat down with the Bevers at their dining room table. Kim got the conversation going.

"How do you handle devotions with your children?" she asked, hearing another squeal of delight ring out in the other room.

"We keep it a secret," replied Susan Bever, with a smile. Kim looked at her quizzically, then Susan added, "We don't let them know they're having devotions!"

"I don't follow you," Dave interjected.

"What Susan is trying to tell you," said Bob Bever, "is that we think in terms of discipling our kids, rather than viewing our task as setting up a special devotional time. We try to consider each day as offering many opportunities for training our children in the Lord."

"Well, sure, I suppose we all do that, but—"

"Actually," Bob said. "Probably few Christian parents do it. Oh, we all claim a desire to raise our children 'in the nurture and admonition of the Lord.' But I know few parents who intentionally plan to train their kids for God, who know exactly what values they want to build into the lives of their children, who have developed a method for instilling those desired qualities, and who follow through on their plan. Most parents do very little intentional training of their kids. We're at least trying to make some progress in those areas."

Dave considered this for a moment. "I see what you mean," he replied. "We all want our kids to love Jesus and to know the Word, but . . . . yeah, I guess I don't know many parents who have a plan for raising their kids. They probably figure it'll just happen."

"I'm beginning to realize, though, that not many things worthwhile just happen."

"You're right."

"We have a basic assumption in our family," Susan Bever said. "We assume that we—Bob and I—are the ones who are ultimately responsible for discipling our children. We must take charge of their spiritual upbringing, and we don't want to leave it to chance. The church can't do it, not in one or two hours a week at Sunday School and Awana. So we've decided on a plan—an architectural design, if you will—for building a home where the kids are growing in Christ."

> "You first have to answer the question: 'What do I want my kids to become'?"

Bob joined in. "That means we have to work at setting an example for them. We try to do a lot of modeling for our kids. But it also means that we, as parents, have to sit down with pencil and paper to discuss exactly what our kids need in order to be learning and growing in their spiritual lives. Then we devise a plan."

"Does that work?" asked Dave, who was surprised to find someone confidently talking about the spiritual nurture of their children.

"Look at the advantages," answered Bob. "First, it allows you to mold your kids, rather than waiting for the world to mold them. Second, it helps your kids develop godly habits and life-styles. Third, this kind of intentional planning creates a cohesive spiritual center for your family."

"Best of all," added Susan, "it brings you the ultimate joy of leading your kids to personal salvation."

"You see, I'm finally starting to understand that I am responsible for training my children, Dave. No one else is. Just me. So we're fulfilling God's command for us as fathers when we disciple our children."

Dave looked at his wife for a minute, mulling over what he had just heard. "Let's suppose somebody wanted to do that in his family," he said, turning toward Bob. "How would he start?"

"Well, I think you first have to answer the question: 'What do I want my kids to become?' You know the old saying, 'If you don't know where you're going, chances are you'll wind up somewhere else!' Where are you going with your girls? What do you want them to be like as adults?"

"Do you mean we need to talk about our expectations of them for the future?" asked Kim.

"Both the near future and the distant future," replied Bob. "You need a vision for what the 'finished product' will look like. A builder doesn't start nailing boards together without a drawing of the home he is building. Think about what qualities and character traits you'd like to see built into your kids."

"When we first started, I'll bet we had seventy or eighty things on our list," laughed Susan. "At that rate, we'd still be discipling them when they're on social security! So we focus on a few important character traits and values we want to instill each year. This year we're hoping to convey the importance of honesty, trustworthiness, and self-control. Last year we spent a lot of time on being a loving, kind, and courteous person."

" 'What do I want my kids to be?'—that's the first question," said Bob. The next logical question is: 'What steps do we need to take to produce that kind of person?' That makes sense, doesn't it? You follow up your plan with a specific strategy. Otherwise, you'd have a goal but no way of attaining it."

"So you sit down and think up ways to build those qualities into your family?" asked Kim, with a look of incredulity on her face.

"It's not that hard, really," said Susan. "My training as a teacher helps considerably, but it isn't like we're spending hours and hours writing lesson plans for them."

At that point the children came racing into the room, pleading at the top of their lungs for a game of hide-and-seek. The two dads motioned for their wives to stay seated, then charged off to the basement with the five girls, the littlest pulling her favorite blanket along behind her. The Bever's youngest, Daniel, had fallen asleep on the couch. Susan checked to see that Grandma and Grandpa were comfortably situated in the living room easy chairs, then she returned to the kitchen, poured two cups of tea, and sat down again.

"Now that you've got me all excited, tell me how you do it!" exclaimed Kim to her friend.

"Well, as I said, it's really not all that difficult," said Susan, stirring her tea. "We begin by choosing a character trait that we feel we need to work on with the kids. Each week we have a theme—usually a "Living Value" from *The Illustrated Bible*—and we look for one Bible story that speaks to that theme-value."

"So you use just one Bible story per week?"

"Yes, usually. Of course, we'll probably read different Bible story books throughout the week, but we try to focus on one story per week. That way the children really get to know the story and the characters involved. The characters are what are most important. If we can find a story about one Bible character that clearly speaks to the trait we are focusing on that week, our work becomes very simple. People like stories about other people, especially if they do something brave or different or silly. For example, when we were working with the girls on the concept of 'revenge', we told them the story of Moses killing the Egyptian. They were able to make the connection that when Moses took revenge he didn't help himself or his people; he only caused more problems. When we were looking at kindness the girls enjoyed hearing about the romance of Ruth and Boaz. People love hearing about people."

"We make it easy on ourselves. Each week we follow a pattern. We have a theme, and we look for one Bible story that speaks to it."

"Maybe that's why 'People' magazine is so popular!" said Kim with a smile.

"We try to use biblical characters and Bible stories each week to teach the kids truth. We also use the calendar, fitting our activities around the Christian days."

"What do you mean?"

"Most of our lives seem to revolve around the calendar. So we look for reasons to celebrate during the year. And we make a real attempt to emphasize Christian days; Christendom should guide our time, not Hallmark. For instance, we celebrate patriotic days, Passion Week, Resurrection Day, All-saints Day, Thanksgiving, Epiphany, and, of course, all the days associated with Christmas. That way we get much more of a focus on God throughout the year. Each week we take our one character value, or our one celebration theme, and build on it."

"What does one of your weeks look like?" asked Kim,

12

anxious to see how it all worked out in practice.

"Once every few months Bob and I take one evening to talk about the girls' development. We discuss the character traits, talk about which Bible characters exemplify the desired values, and select appropriate Bible stories. In an hour or so we have the basis of the next several months figured out. We just make a list that looks like this:

January: Honesty
Bible character: Jacob
Bible stories: Jacob's blessing; tricking Isaac; getting tricked by Laban.

February: Courage
Bible character: Joshua
Bible stories: Entering the land; taking Jericho; conquering the promised land.

March: Obedience
Bible character: various
Bible stories: Adam, Noah, Jonah.

"You see? It only takes a little while to get our basic outline together. Then we note the special celebration days we want to observe, let's say New Years, Presidents Day, and Valentines Day. Our basic calendar is done for three months."

"And it just comes to you," said Kim, shaking her head. "You make it sound easy."

"It is simple, although perhaps not easy. But good things take time. However, yes, as we talk about it, it just comes to us. We discuss a character trait, or Living Value, and then think of appropriate Bible stories. Then we sit down every Sunday afternoon, during our 'down time.' We make sure the kids are playing or napping, the guests have gone home, the

13

football game hasn't gone into overtime, and we chat for about fifteen minutes. We have already agreed on the theme for the week, so all we have to do is talk through the week's activities."

"But isn't it very difficult thinking up a bunch of devotions for the week?"

"There you go again, talking about devotions!" Susan said with a laugh. "Did I say anything about devotions? If we told the girls we were having devotions, they'd probably think it was something awful! We just have fun, plan activities, and live our lives. We simply have one story, around which many of the week's activities will be planned."

"All right, but where do you get your ideas for activities?"

"We make it easy on ourselves. Each week we follow a pattern. Here," Susan reached for a piece of paper and handed it to Kim. "This is our planning chart."

Living Value for the week:
(Special celebration day):
Scripture:
Character:
Memory verse:
Materials needed:

SUNDAY: Introduce the topic
MONDAY: Do a simple activity
TUESDAY: Tell a story
WEDNESDAY: Offer a self-esteem builder
THURSDAY: Enjoy worship together
FRIDAY: Do another simple activity
SATURDAY: Have a special event

SUNDAY: A TOPIC INTRODUCTION
"Each Sunday afternoon we talk through our week. First,

14

we decide on a good way to introduce the topic. We always introduce the topic to the girls on Sunday evening, as we're eating, or playing a game, or giving them a bath. This isn't anything very difficult; it's usually a question or a little story that causes them to think about the topic. For example, if we're going to be looking for honesty, I might say to Bob in front of the kids, 'Have you ever told a lie? What happened?' Then Bob will tell us some story about his life."

"And that's all you do to introduce it?" inquired Kim. "No big classes or craft projects?"

"Heavens no, not on Sunday!" Susan laughed as she replied. "We're all ready for a relaxing evening before the start of another week. Sometimes Sundays can wear us all out. We try to make Sunday a day of rest, so our evening includes just a brief mention of the week's theme. There is no use giving them another Sunday School class. Besides, we've got all week to work on it."

"So what comes next?"

MONDAY: A SIMPLE ACTIVITY

"Well, as Bob and I talk through the week, we decide on a simple activity for Monday. That might mean we play a game, take a photo, or color a picture."

"How does that relate to your week's theme?"

"The activity we select usually has some connection. For example, when our value was 'obedience,' we played fol-low-the-leader with the children. This week was our anniversary, so for our Monday activity we took a picture of the family. You see, it doesn't have to be anything terribly complex, it just has to relate to the topic in some way. What we are doing is supporting the week's theme through simple activities, but at the same time we are having fun, building family unity, and, perhaps most importantly, showing the kids how Christians are to live."

"Showing them how to live?"

"Sure. We find that, as a family, we don't just naturally play together. Our only contact often happens when we're sitting around the TV at the same time. But when we're working our plan, we want our kids to see how Christians play, to see how families play, so that they'll grow up valuing 'fun.' Then, we're not just taking them through devotions, we're discipling them; we're showing them how Christians live."

"And a game of hide-and-seek accomplishes that?"

"Kim, I'll tell you something. Any man that plays hide-and-seek with his children on a weekly basis will probably be nominated for Best Daddy of the Year by his kids. Bob and I try to show the girls that Christianity isn't something we just 'do' on Sundays. Christianity is something we live all week long. So we want to show the girls how a Christian goes grocery shopping, how a Christian does the laundry, how a Christian cleans the house—there is no end to the ways you can think about discipling your kids."

"I never thought of doing laundry as a discipleship opportunity!" laughed Kim. "Maybe I should disciple Dave!"

"You know, Bob once took the girls into his office so they could see how a Christian man behaves at work. He also takes them on 'dates' occasionally so they'll recognize a gentleman when they're old enough to date. Modern-day Christians are stuck on the idea of discipleship as 'teaching,' but the word can better be understood as 'mentoring' or 'apprenticing.' We want to determine how our daughters will be shaped, so we apprentice them into the Christian life."

TUESDAY: A STORY TIME

"Let's go back to the planning sheet for a minute," said Kim, picking up the sheet and examining it. "On Tuesdays you usually tell your kids the Bible story?"

"Yes. But I emphasize the word 'TELL.' Sometimes I'll read it from a Bible, sometimes Sarah will read it from her children's Bible. Sometimes Bob will just tell the girls the story, or we'll ask the girls to tell it back to us. Often we act it out, and of course the girls will want to repeat it over and over; you know how kids love repetition. We've used puppets and pictures and flannelgraphs, but usually we just tell it, the Bible story that we've selected for the week. Sometimes we just tell a story from our personal lives that helps illustrate the week's theme."

> "We look for something called 'the teachable moment.' It means being ready for those crucial few seconds when a kid really wants to *know*."

WEDNESDAY: A SELF-ESTEEM BUILDER

"So by Wednesday they've thought about the topic, done an activity related to it, and heard a Bible story about it."

"That's right," said Susan. "And on Wednesday we do a bit of a departure. We focus on self-esteem."

"I noticed that. Why?"

"Poor self-esteem is so common among children these days. Perhaps it's because children can be so brutal to one another; they'll just tear each other to pieces at school. We worried about the impact on our girls, so we're trying to do something about it."

"What do you do?"

"Every Wednesday we make a point of doing something to build up our children psychologically. Sometimes we play a game in which we get to remind them of their best qualities, or we'll award trophies for special things they've done, or we may just reinforce the fact that they are pretty, lovable, and worthwhile."

17

"It sounds like a lot of work," said Kim, thinking about how she was going to fit all of this into an already over-booked schedule.

"It isn't really. As I said, Bob and I come up with simple little ideas during our short talks on Sunday afternoons. The self-esteem activities are usually very simple to think up— we just ask ourselves, 'How does my son need to be encouraged this week?' 'What are his strengths and how could I reinforce them?' Don't make this harder than it really is. So far all we've done is tell one story and played a few fun games."

"So far?"

THURSDAY: A FAMILY WORSHIP TIME

"Yes, because once a week we have a more complex time. We set aside Thursday nights for family worship time. That is the night that you probably think of as a 'devotional' time. But we don't have typical devotions. We make a point of using that time to help the kids understand and begin to apply the Living Value we're working on.

"For instance, when we were working on developing patience a few months back, we all sat down together and talked briefly about what the word 'patience' means. I told the kids about some times I've been impatient. Sarah retold our Bible story. Bob played a song from a Christian album called 'Patience.' Then everyone took a pencil and wrote on a sheet of paper one way to show patience. We exchanged papers and prayed for each other. Now our entire time took, maybe, twelve or fourteen minutes. But it included Scripture, prayer, and personal application to our lives. It was short, fun, and focused on our theme. In a couple of weeks we'll be talking about honesty and how we need to tell the truth even when it seems safer to lie. For the Bible story, we're using Daniel's three friends and the fiery furnace. Our family worship night will

18

include a wienie roast over a hot fire, and a pretend TV interview with Shadrach, Meshach, and Abednigo. That night took us maybe ten minutes to plan."

Kim looked at her friend in admiration. "I don't think I've got the creativity to think up great ideas like that every week."

"You don't have to," Susan said. "There are a number of good books that you can find at a Christian book store that will give you ideas. We've used Wayne Rickerson's *Family Fun Times* and Evelyn Blitchington's *The Family Devotions Idea Book*. We learned quite a bit from Mary White's *Successful Family Devotions*. Gloria Gaither and Shirley Dobson collaborated on an excellent book entitled *Let's Make a Memory*, and Carolyn Williford has a great book out called *Devotions for Families That Can't Sit Still*. That idea for the TV interview

> **"Here I was, trying to sell my little girl on the value of Bible reading, and all she ever saw me reading was the newspaper."**

came from the last book. The important thing is not your own unique creativity, it's your *adaptive* creativity. As you read about some good ideas, you'll think of ways to adapt them for your own use in your particular situation."

"Tell me the truth, Susan, does this work for you?"

"I'd say it works pretty well most of the time. And it's not that hard. It takes commitment to disciple your children, but once you make that commitment, you've taken the biggest step."

FRIDAY: ANOTHER SIMPLE ACTIVITY

"Tell me about the rest of the week," Kim said, noticing

that the fathers were bringing the kids back up from their game.

"Friday is very simple. Once again, we pick a game or an easy activity to do with the kids. It's the end of the week, everybody is tired, and we just had our worship night on Thursday, so we keep this activity very simple, just like on Monday nights. We might play a board game or twenty questions, anything fun and easy."

"How does that contribute to discipling?"

"It puts us together as a family, having fun. That's a rare enough event in our world, I'd say."

SATURDAY: A SPECIAL EVENT

Susan put the cups in the sink and continued. "Saturday we always plan some special event. Don't get the wrong idea, it's not always a *big* event, it's just something out of the ordinary. Last week we went swimming. Today we had Grandpa and Grandma visit us. Next week we're going to surprise the kids with an indoor picnic. Often our conversation will drift around to our theme for the week, and we'll ask the kids to act out the week's story, or tell us how they're going to put it into practice. We try to have some intentionality to our time together, but we don't lose sleep over it not being 'deep' enough."

"Is it hard to stick to a weekly schedule like this?" asked Kim, looking again at the Bevers' planning sheet.

"Not really. We try to stay with our schedule because it covers the scope and sequence of our discipling plan, but we feel free to change a lesson, or even drop it entirely if something else comes up—or if Bob and I are too tired or tied up with other things. Our kids do know that we're not perfect! But our theme gives us focus for the week, and we feel that frees us from constantly having to dream up new ideas."

The children were standing around the table now, hoping Mom would get the hint and make them some hot chocolate. As Kim rose to help, Susan continued, "We look for something called 'the teachable moment.' It means being ready for those crucial few seconds when a kid really wants to *know*. Having a theme for the week makes the teachable moments much easier to recognize.

"Who wants some hot cocoa?" Hands went up everywhere, and Susan began pouring milk into a pan. Bob and Dave peeled away from the mob of bobbing heads and made their way to two chairs in the den.

❦

**"You need to know your purpose
—and have a plan for accomplishing it."**

"I'd like to talk more about how you disciple your kids," said Dave, settling back into his chair. "There's so much to it; so many things to consider."

"My wife would tell you you're making it too complicated," Bob responded. "Discipling children isn't all that confusing. I guess you need to know your purpose; that is, what you are trying to accomplish, and you need a plan for accomplishing it. When I think about it in those terms, it becomes like any other sort of project. You want some hot chocolate?" Bob moved to rise from his chair, but Dave stopped him.

"No, thanks. What I'd really like is to know how you developed your plan."

"I think our wives were discussing that very thing while we were down in the basement. Susan probably has been filling up your wife's head with all kinds of creative ideas. She's like that."

Dave nodded. "We've tried it before. Family devotions, I mean. We'll insist that everyone sit down, we'll read some Scripture, maybe do some singing, pray for people . . . but

21

it never 'clicks,' do you know what I mean? We're never able to make it fun or exciting or whatever it's supposed to be."

"I know what that's like. We tried that for quite a while with our eldest child, Sarah, but it always wound up with me frustrated and Sarah bored."

"What made the difference?"

"When we realized we were trying to make our home into a Sunday School. Sarah didn't need that; she's got a Sunday School. And they probably do it better than I ever could! Instead, Sarah needed a model."

"A model?"

"That's right, a model. An example of what a Christian is. Someone who could tell her, 'This is the pattern, imitate what I'm doing.' She wasn't getting that. Or at least she was getting the wrong pattern."

"Really?"

"Don't misunderstand me. Susan and I loved the Lord and desired to raise godly kids, we just didn't know how to encourage a devotional life in them. Then one day I heard a preacher say, 'You can't give away what you don't have.' It hit me. Here I was, trying to sell my little girl on the value of Bible reading, and all she ever saw me reading was the newspaper. Or maybe a western. I wanted her to grasp the importance of prayer, but my life showed her that it was only important to pray before eating or in an emergency. She was going to grow up thinking God was confined to Sunday mornings, Christmas, and the dinner table. So the first thing I did was to start reading my Bible a little more, especially at times when Sarah would notice. I started praying with her every day, not just at the table, either. And you know what?" Bob gave a wide smile. "My life changed, which was probably the best thing I could have done for my family."

"And that's what made the difference in your family

devotions?"

"Well . . . maybe not at first. But I began discovering things in God's Word that I wanted to tell someone. So I started telling my family. Pretty soon we weren't forcing everyone to sit down and be quiet so we could have this thing called 'devotions.' We were just talking about God. Who He is. What He had done. What He has said. How He wants us to live. And everything grew out of that."

Bob waited, letting his words sink in for a minute, then he began explaining in more detail. "Susan and I have come up with seven 'building blocks' that we think are crucial for every family to include in the foundation of their discipling plan. Do you want to hear them?"

"Absolutely."

> **"If this is the way we're supposed to be discipling our kids, and if it works like you say, how come nobody is doing it?"**

BUILDING BLOCK #1: STORIES

"First, you've got to give children stories. Kids love stories, especially the same stories told again and again. You know why? Because stories, particularly familiar stories, help them understand their world. Stories explain things, create vistas, shrink the world into pieces a child can understand. So parents need to read to their kids. Read all kinds of things: Bibles, books, picture books, activity books, magazines, everything. And don't stop when your children learn to read, keep reading to them. It brings a closeness and a shared world that is hard to get in any other way.

"You can find some excellent story books for children at any Christian book store—not the simple story lines of most picture books, mind you, but books with plenty of stories and parables that will enrich your child's imagination and cause her to think. We also use children's Bibles, Gil Beers' *My Picture Bible* and Ken Taylor's *The Bible in Pictures for Little Eyes.* The older kids like Dave and Neta Jackson's *Best Loved Bible Stories* and Ray Hughes' *Illustrated Bible Stories for Children.*

"Have your kids read stories to you sometimes. It will make them feel important, and it will improve their reading skills. Read them a story every night before bedtime, and talk about the story so that you are sure they're comprehending what's happening. Read them the Bible, and make sure they see you reading the Bible on your own.

"Read great books to them. Don't always settle for simple, easy readers. Share *The Chronicles of Narnia* and *Little House on the Prairie.* Give them some Dickens and A. A. Milne. Go to the library; it's a golden age for children's writings.

"Don't stop with reading. *Tell* them stories. Tell them about your family, your life, your childhood, their birth, the world, everything. Children need to learn facts, and they learn facts best through stories. Later on you can move from facts to concepts, and eventually you'll teach them how concepts get translated into personal applications. But first start with facts, and facts are what you give through stories."

"Okay," replied Dave. "I can start telling them stories. What else?"

BUILDING BLOCK #2: DINNERS

"The second component of family discipling is dinner together. Make it a priority to eat together every day. It will bond your family and give you the chance to stay in contact with each other, which isn't easy any more. We try to fill up our meal times with conversation: jokes, what we're all learning, family stories, Bible quizzes, the list is endless. Did you know that Rose Kennedy used to write a topic on a chalkboard every day, and at the evening meal everyone was expected to be prepared to discuss it? She turned out a bunch of kids who knew their world! After stories, dinner is the next important ingredient."

"I follow you," said Dave, who was taking notes. "Stories and dinners. What else?"

BUILDING BLOCK #3: PRAYER

"The next two essential ingredients for discipling your kids are prayer and Scripture memorization. Prayer because kids need to know that they can talk with God. Bible memorization because they need to think about Him. We've tried all kinds of things with prayer. We use pictures, lists, notebooks, prayer projects, letters from missionaries, you name it. We'll pray in different positions, using different words. Sometimes we use the ACTS—Adoration / Confession / Thanksgiving / Supplication—format, other times we don't. We mix it up, and for a good reason—prayer is talking with God. That's what we want our kids to understand. Just as you and I will vary our conversations, so we don't always go to God in the same way. God isn't an impersonal force 'out there,' He is a personal being who lives here in our home with us. We reverence Him, but we can go to Him and talk at any time.

"It's important also to make sure you pray *for* something. I see parents who never really pray for anything. 'Make Johnny well.' 'Give us a safe trip.' We know those things are safe, so we pray for them. We're trying to pray more specifically. Evelyn Blitchington once said, 'If God is not a prayer-answering God, aren't we better to find it out right now, and have done with this pious nonsense? If God can't be approached with our everyday needs, aren't we better off to discover it right now, so that our children can be spared the hypocrisy and futility of believing in an all-powerful God who never lifts a finger?' Praying with my kids, and letting them see me pray is essential to my discipling plan.

BUILDING BLOCK #4: SCRIPTURE MEMORIZATION

"Scripture memorizing is important because it is through that process children learn the Word of God. The Bible makes a lot of promises about itself—that those who memorize it will find guidance, growth, and a safeguard from sin. Doesn't that sound wonderful? Who wouldn't want that for their children? We take a verse or two every month and plaster them all over the house—on the refrigerator, in lunchsacks, in the bathroom, everywhere. And we check with each other to make sure everyone is held accountable. I learn them, and it has been wonderful to be learning new Scripture truths! The key is to repeat, review, and reinforce every verse."

Bob stopped for a minute. "Am I giving you too much? This might be a little like trying to get a drink out of a fire hose."

"No," replied Dave. "This is just what I need. Give me the rest."

BUILDING BLOCK #5: MUSIC

"All right. Another important aspect of family discipling is music. Now, to tell you the truth, I'm not terribly musical. Susan is, so that helps considerably, but I'm convinced that the greatest aid to family music is the tape player. Pick up some copies of the Maranatha Kids Praise tapes. Two other good resources are the Wee Sing tapes and "GT and the Halo Express." Our kids can't get enough of 'The Donut Man' tapes, which are Bible stories put to music. Filling your home with music throughout the day is both biblical and enjoyable. A family that can learn to sing together will discover a great bonding occurs through their music. I've had fun Christmas carolling before, but last year when our family went out carolling together was the best time I ever had singing."

BUILDING BLOCK #6: HOSPITALITY

Our children need exposure to other people, other cultures, and other ideas. They've met many other Christians around our dinner table. They've heard tales of God at work in people's everyday lives. We try to have people over regularly, and the kids have begun to see how Christians treat other people.

Let this proud Papa tell you a story: Last month we had missionaries stay the weekend with us. After hearing of all the joys and struggles they experienced in their ministry, Sarah said to me, 'Dad, I'm going to try to be more of a missionary at my school.'"

"That's great. I'd love to have my girls think that thought."

"Well, let me give you the last building block for a discipling plan, then we'll go back and join the crowd. The seventh component on our list is simply: time."

BUILDING BLOCK #7: TIME

"We use lots of our 'down time' just to be with the kids. Little Daniel helps me wash the car, and we talk. Emily helps her mom sort laundry, and they talk. I'll play a little football or baseball in the backyard with the kids, we get a chance to wrestle around with each other, and they see Christ in me. I'm not saying I'm a perfect dad, either, it's just that they get to see how Christians live in this world from being with Susan and me. They get to see our successes and how we handle our failures. And I'd rather they learned how to live from watching me than from watching the tube. There's just no substitute for spending time with your kids.

27

"I try to be sure that the time we spend is not just all talking or teaching verbally. I want my kids to be sure that I love them, and kids need to *feel* that they are loved as well as *know* it. So both Susan and I make a point of touching and holding the kids in appropriate ways. Sometimes we just sit and hold them quietly for a while, letting them fill their emotional tanks in silence. I can't tell you how much I wish my own parents would have done more of that with me. And I can't really think of an age that a person outgrows the need for that kind of affection from parents."

Dave sat and looked at his list. "Thanks. Thanks a lot, you've really helped me get a handle on this."

"Well, try it out for a while and see how it goes. I'm guessing your family's way of doing it will be different from mine, but if this helps a little bit, great." After talking more about kids, rain, and the Green Bay Packers, they got up and joined the others in the dining room. The children were playing a game in the family room, and Kim and Susan were standing in the kitchen, discussing activities to try with their children.

"If they find it boring," Susan was saying while mopping up the cocoa rings on the counter, "I figure it's because the activities were either too easy, too hard, or too much the same."

"That's right," added the kids' Grandma, joining in the discussion. "When Bobby was a little guy and we had devotions, his sister thought she was too grown up for all of it. She liked the games and many of the activities, but she didn't want anything to do with the 'little kid' songs and worship activities. They were too easy!"

"So what did you do?" asked Dave.

"We asked her to help lead us! And sometimes we'd have a one-on-one discussion with her, after we'd had our time with the little ones. Those discussions sure came in handy after she became a teenager!"

"I suppose the attitude of the kids is pretty important?" asked Kim as she put water in the last of the dirty cups.

"Not nearly as much as the attitude of the parents," responded Susan. "If you approach them and say, 'I've got an idea, this will be fun!', they're bound to catch your enthusiasm."

"You know, there is one thing I just don't understand in all of this," Dave admitted to the group. "If this is the way we're supposed to be discipling our kids, and if it works like you say, how come nobody is doing it?"

"I think a lot of folks are just too undisciplined to do it," replied Bob's mother. "It takes a lot of work to decide you're going to build Christian values into the lives of your kids."

"Many parents are probably just too busy," Susan added. "I don't know anybody with time on their hands any more. Busyness seems to be the bane of the modern Christian's existence."

"Boy, I'll say," chimed in Kim. "My schedule is full; there is always something planned for church or school. I feel like I'm constantly under time pressure."

"Yes, and when you finally get some free time, you just want to drop everything."

"Our decision to disciple our kids was very difficult in that regard," said Bob. "In essence, we were telling the world that our kids took precedence over our committees. We stopped running around every night. Our pace slowed down."

"Really, the reason we moved to Portland was because of the children," added Susan. "Bob's old job kept him out late most nights, and he was gone quite a bit to conferences and workshops. He took a new job here because he wanted to make sure he spent more time at home. We do much more as a family now, and we seem to be living life at a slower pace."

"I figured I had my whole life to work, but only a few years to shape my kids," admitted Bob.

"Still, I can think of one major obstacle for us to hurdle as we started discipleship with the children," said Kim, looking at her husband.

"What's that, hon?"

"Television."

"That's a real problem," admitted Susan. "As a former teacher, I have a very low view of TV. There is no interaction, it blocks conversation, shortens attention spans, and dulls creativity. Still, even I struggled with the idea of missing my favorite programs."

"What did you do?" asked Kim.

"We considered selling it, or at least putting it in the closet where it would take a major effort to get it out," said Bob. "We finally decided on a solution that works for us."

"Everyone gets to pick one show a week to watch. Mom has editorial control," added Susan.

"I even limit myself to one football game per week," said Bob. "Although I make it a late one so I can catch the highlights of the ones I've missed."

"We will occasionally rent a videotape, but only if Bob and I have watched it beforehand. And we *insist* that at the end of the program everyone discuss what they've just watched. That way we get some amount of interaction and intellectual stimulation."

"You know, we've had plenty of intellectual stimulation tonight," Dave said to Bob and Susan. "It's getting close to bedtime, so we're going to take the girls home now, but I want to say thanks. We really appreciate your taking the time to talk with us."

"It was our pleasure," said Bob. "We love to talk with people about discipling kids." He pulled the Andersons' coats from the closet and passed them out. "And now that you know what we're trying to do, we hope you'll discover some new things that work and share your ideas with us."

❦

"If we don't do it, then who will?"

"What do you think?" Dave asked his wife as they sat on the couch later. "Can we do it?"

"Dave, I want our girls to grow into godly women. I always wanted to be a mother, and now that I am one . . . I want to do it right."

"You know it will mean making some changes? I mean, TV, church work, all of that?"

"Who else is going to disciple them?"

"Good point," Dave said after a pause. "Who else?"

WEEK 1

Living Value for the Week: COMMITMENT (To personal and family goals)
Special Celebration Day (optional): New Year's Day
Scripture: Psalm 147
Memory Verse: *"Commit your way to the Lord; trust in him and he will do this."—Psalm 37:5*

Materials:
    camera and film
    old magazines
    scrapbook
    scissors, glue
    family photos
    family mementos
    Ping-Pong ball
    masking tape
    calendar

Consider the postage stamp, my son. It secures success through its ability to stick to one thing till it gets there.— Josh Billings

SUNDAY—A Topic Introduction

Ask, and discuss together: "What things do you hope will happen in the year ahead?"

-in our personal lives?
-in our family?
-in our schools and work places?
-in our church?
-in our neighborhood?

MONDAY—A Simple Activity

Take pictures of your family and display them in a prominent place. Talk about the commitment it takes—through exercise, nutrition, and rest—to keep growing bigger and stronger each year.

TUESDAY— A Story Time
Read Psalm 147 verse by verse. Using magazines, ask your kids to find pictures that represent some aspect of each verse.

WEDNESDAY—A Self-esteem Builder
Ask everybody to complete this sentence for another family member: "One neat thing you did/accomplished last year was . . .". Parents go first. After everyone has spoken, discuss what forms of commitment led to the accomplishments.

THURSDAY—A Family Worship Time
Create a family scrapbook, with everyone helping. Make sure to include photo's you took during the past year. Put in some special memento's from vacations, holidays, sports events, birthdays, any special times. You can glue in Christmas and birthday cards, poems that you wrote, even schoolwork and award certificates. Talk about your past year as you work.

FRIDAY—Another Simple Activity
Play "Blow Hockey." Put two pieces of tape four inches apart on each end of your kitchen table. Form two teams, positioned around the table. Blow the "Ping-Pong puck" thru each other's goals. Talk about the commitment it takes to be a good athlete.

SATURDAY—A Special Event
Plan your calendar for the New Year. Sit at the table and mark in holidays, vacations, visits, and special events together. Let everyone make suggestions for things they would like to do in the year ahead. Make sure to set some "family goals" for the year.

PARENTING SUGGESTION: This year consider a resolution to limit your family's television watching to two nights per week. (This would include Mom and Dad, too!)

WEEK 2

Living Value for the Week: HONESTY (By telling the truth)
Character: Daniel
Scripture: Daniel 1
Memory Verse: *"A truthful witness gives honest testimony, but a false witness tells lies." —Proverbs 12:17*

Materials: tennis ball
                  string
                  umbrella, or yardstick
                  pencils
                  index cards
                  paper
                  sing-along records or tapes
                  hymnbooks or music books

Honesty pays, but it doesn't seem to pay enough to suit some people.— Kin Hubbard

SUNDAY—A Topic Introduction

Parents: Have you ever been caught telling a lie? Tell your children about what happened. What did you learn?

MONDAY—A Simple Activity

Play indoor golf. Tie loops of string and put one in each room of your home to serve as "holes." Using an umbrella—upside down—as your club, hit the tennis ball around the house into each hole. Keep score—accurately and honestly!

TUESDAY— A Story Time

Read Daniel 1:1-21. Ask, and discuss: "How did things work out for Daniel when he was truthful about his desire to avoid the king's food?" Emphasize that Daniel could have acted as though he enjoyed the rich diet, just to avoid offending the king.

WEDNESDAY—A Self-esteem Builder

"What is your favorite book? Movie? Television program? Activity?" Make a list of your kids' responses for future reference.

THURSDAY—A Family Worship Time

Before your time together, print portions of Proverbs 12:17 on index cards, one for each member of your family. For example, the first card could say, "A truthful . . . ". Sit in a circle and have a short time of prayer. Distribute the cards (give Dad the first card). All color their names on their cards. Go around the circle and practice saying the verse, each person taking his or her part, until you can all repeat it without looking. Then see who can say the entire verse alone. (Make it easy for small ones!)

FRIDAY—Another Simple Activity

Put slips of paper in a bowl with written entries on them like: "My Best Day," "My Worst Day," "My Dumbest Mistake," "My Greatest Accomplishment." Pass the bowl and have everyone draw a slip and tell, honestly, how they felt in the particular situation.

SATURDAY—A Special Event

Have a sing-along. The youngest gets to pick the first song, then go around the circle asking for more favorites. Sing to tapes or records if that is helpful. You can even turn this into a "family concert" by having solo's and musical numbers.

RESOURCE SUGGESTION: You can find many good children's activities and ideas in Canfield and Wells' 100 Ways to Enhance Self-Concept in the Classroom.

WEEK 3

Living Value for the Week: TRUSTWORTHINESS
Character: Daniel
Scripture: Daniel 2:1-49
Memory Verse: *"Whoever can be trusted with very little can also be trusted with much."—Luke 16:10a*

Materials: a small, handmade trophy
                picnic basket
                tablecloth
                paper cups and plates

What is more lonely than distrust?

SUNDAY—A Topic Introduction
Play "The Trust Fall." Stand behind your children, one at a time. Ask them to close their eyes and fall backward, keeping a straight back. Naturally, you catch them before they crash-land. Ask, and discuss: "How hard is it to trust someone? Who is easy to trust? Who is hard to trust? Can *you* be trusted? Why?"

MONDAY—A Simple Activity
"Trust me!"—Play follow-the-leader through the house, garage, or outdoors. Form a line with everyone holding hands and closing eyes behind the leader. Have each person be the leader for at least one minute. Later, talk about who was trustworthy (who didn't lead others to stumble or bump into things).

TUESDAY— A Story Time
Tell the story of Daniel 2:1-49, then do a mock TV interview with Daniel, the king, and a bystander. Ask kids to think up questions they would want to ask these people. Discuss: "How hard do you think it was for Daniel to trust God and tell the king the truth about the dream? Why?"

You may wish to tell about a time when you experienced God as being trustworthy.

WEDNESDAY—A Self-esteem Builder
Watch for a time when your child displays trustworthiness by following through on your instructions without being watched. Surprise him or her with a "Trustworthy Trophy." (To make the trophy, use an old bowling trophy, or make a new one from a small box and a toy figure. Put the words "Trustworthy Trophy" on it.)

THURSDAY—A Family Worship Time
Set up an obstacle course in your living room. Place pillows, toys, and chairs around the room, leaving one wiggly path through the obstacles. Dad goes first: Blindfold him and have one child talk him through it without touching Dad. Each person, one at a time, walks through the course. Time each person to see who makes it through fastest.

Afterwards, discuss the activity: "How hard was this? Who trusted the 'guide'? Who didn't trust? Why? Did I tell you the truth? How is life like an obstacle course? Where can we find truth and guidance that won't let us down?"

FRIDAY—Another Simple Activity
Show your child how to do a simple chore around the house—like washing the dishes. Give complete instructions, and then leave for awhile. Come back, ready to give praise for trustworthiness.

SATURDAY—A Special Event
Announce to your family that tonight you're having a "winter picnic." Put chicken legs, potato salad, and other picnic items, into a picnic basket, spread out a table cloth on the floor (in front of a window or fireplace), and enjoy yourselves. Use paper plates so there will be little clean-up.

RESOURCE SUGGESTION: A great book for families who enjoy allegories and parables that teach Christian values is David and Karen Mains' *Tales of the Kingdom* **(Chariot).**

37

WEEK 4

Living Value for the Week: SELF-DISCIPLINE (To stand firm against opposition)
Character: Daniel
Scripture: Daniel 3
Memory Verse: *"We must obey God rather than men!"—Acts 5:29b*

Materials: crayons
                pencils and paper
                a puzzle

Attempt something so great for God that it's doomed to failure unless God be in it.

SUNDAY—A Topic Introduction
Tell your kids about a time when, as a child, you had to stand up for something you believed in, even though others were against you. Discuss: "What's hard, and what's good, about not always going along with everybody else?"

MONDAY—A Simple Activity
Play "Mimic the Master." Stand in a circle. One child leaves and you choose a Master, who does a series of silly motions that the others must follow. The child returns and tries to guess who the Master is. Talk about what it takes to follow God even when others may be against us.

TUESDAY— A Story Time
Tell what happened in Daniel 3:1-30. Have smaller kids act out the action as you tell the story. Discuss: "How would you have felt if a king told you to stop worshiping God? What would you do?"

WEDNESDAY—A Self-esteem Builder

Give your kids paper and pencil. Have them write a story with themselves as the heroes (younger ones can simply tell their stories). Ask them to draw a picture of themselves doing the brave deeds in their stories.

THURSDAY—A Family Worship Time

Tonight is Grown-up Night. First, ask your children to set the table. Then, give them simple recipes and tell them they will be cooking dinner tonight! Use some easy menus, like bacon and eggs or beef stew. Let them go at it—the lesson will be worth the mess! After dinner, guide them through washing the dishes, sorting the laundry, emptying the trash, and sewing on buttons. During these activities, talk with the children about the importance of fulfilling responsibilities even when they may feel like quitting.

FRIDAY—Another Simple Activity

Have the whole family work on a puzzle. Stress the importance of doing things the right way. Take time to work on your memory verse.

SATURDAY—A Special Event

After your kids are bathed and just tucked in for bed, burst into their room and yell, "Pajama ride!" Put their coats on, get in the car, and go out for an ice cream cone. The kids will remember this surprise forever.

RESOURCE SUGGESTION: For a fine children's book (ages eight and up) teaching self-discipline, consider *Mystery on Mirror Mountain* (Chariot).

WEEK 5

Living Value for the Week: TRUST (Trusting God)
Character: Daniel
Scripture: Daniel 4:1-37
Memory Verse: *"In you our fathers put their trust; they trusted and you delivered them."—Psalm 22:4*

Materials: crayons
paper
pencils
balloons
paints

If you seek to please God, you'll please the people who count.

SUNDAY—A Topic Introduction
Ask: "Has God ever answered our prayers? When? How?" Tell a story about a specific answer to prayer in your life.

MONDAY—A Simple Activity
Paint pictures of a "trustworthy" car (or plane, or boat) and an "untrustworthy" car. Ask and discuss: "Which one would you rather ride in? How is God like, and unlike, a trustworthy car?"

TUESDAY—A Story Time
Read Daniel 4, the story of King Nebuchadnezzar. After reading it, ask your kids to retell it back to you.

WEDNESDAY—A Self-esteem Builder
Give each child pencil and paper. Ask them to list ten things they want to do in their lives (fly a plane, be a mommy, teach school, play for the Green Bay Packers). Pray with them, that

God will give thme wisdom and strength to trust Him always. Stress that God can be trusted to guide them into their futures.

THURSDAY—A Family Worship Time

The Family Theater presents: "The Braggy King of Babylon." Starring: Your Children.

Have your children dress up in their bathrobes, with towel-turbans on their heads. One child will play the king, another will play Daniel, everybody else will be the people who drive the king away. Present the play for Dad, grandparents, or neighbors and friends. Later, talk about the meaning of the story. Be sure to tell the kids what a great job they did as actors.

FRIDAY—Another Simple Activity

Play balloon games: keep a balloon off the floor; play volley-balloon; or try indoor footballoon (points are scored when the balloon is batted over an opponent's "goal"—made of couch pillows). Talk about how God does not "keep us up in the air" when we need comfort, guidance, protection.

SATURDAY—A Special Event

Take a trip to the snow (or, in warm climates, to the beach or woods). Go sledding, make snowmen and snow angels (or find interesting leaves, rocks, shells) and talk about the greatness and wonder of God's creation. In the car on the way back, talk about how King Nebuchadnezzar got a vision of God's greatness.

RESOURCE SUGGESTION: Chariot Books has published a great Bible story book entitled *Best Loved Bible Stories*. It's our family's favorite.

WEEK 6

Living Value for the Week: courage (In the face of physical danger)
Character: Daniel
Scripture: Daniel 6:1-28
Memory Verse: *"Take courage! It is I. Don't be afraid."*—Mark 6:50b

Materials: stuffed animals
     a piece of paper, balled up
     paper and pencils
     two tennis balls

Courage in people is like a tea bag. You never know the strength until they're in hot water.

SUNDAY—A Topic Introduction

Tell your kids about a time when you were in physical danger. Were you afraid? What helped you pull through it?

MONDAY—A Simple Activity

Play hide and seek. Ask smaller children how afraid they would be if a lion were seeking for them? What would help them be less afraid and more brave?

TUESDAY—A Story Time

Tell your children the story of Daniel in the lion's den. Have the kids sit in a circle to retell the story, using the "throw and catch" method. Toss a balled-up piece of paper to a kid, who throws it back and tells part of the story until you throw the paper to someone else. The new catcher throws the paper back to you and takes up the story . . . and so on.

WEDNESDAY—A Self-esteem Builder

Around the dinner table, give everyone a round sheet of paper and a pencil. Have kids write their names on the papers. Now pass them to the left, and everyone writes what they appreciate about the one whose name is written in the center. Keep passing the papers until they return to their owners. Read them aloud.

Ask the group to think about ways they have seen family members display courage. Talk about how God helps us when we're afraid.

THURSDAY—A Family Worship Time

Begin by singing a song (you can find some good ones about Daniel in the lion's den). Take your stuffed "lions" and act out the story of Daniel, the king, and the lion's den. Your kids might want to act out the story several times, trading parts each time.

Follow this with a short role play: Dad pretends to be a bad boy and tries to talk your children into doing something wrong (lie, hit sister, steal something). Have your kids practice their responses. Close by praying for strength and courage in situations of temptation.

FRIDAY—Another Simple Activity

Play Crash Tennis. Place one team at the ends of a table, the other at the sides. The Ends Team tries to roll a tennis ball the length of the table, the Sides Team tries to prevent it by rolling the other ball into the first ball. (The first ball must be rolled slowly enough for a count to three before it reaches the other end of the table.)

SATURDAY—A Special Event

Ask Grandpa and Grandma (or other relative or close friend) over for an evening visit. Ask them to tell what you—the parents—were like as a child. (If Grandparents can't be invited, consider asking older Christians to come over and tell what life was like when they were growing up.) Talk about scary or dangerous situations that were survived.

RESOURCE SUGGESTION: Your family will love James Herriott's books. For instance: *All Creatures Great and Small*, *All Things Bright and Beautiful*.

WEEK 7

Living Value for the Week: LOVING
Special Celebration Day (optional): Valentine's Day
Scripture: I Corinthians 13:4-7
Memory Verse: *"Dear friends, since God so loved us, we also ought to love one another."—I John 4:11*

Materials: a copy of the book, The Velveteen Rabbit
toilet paper and tube
pens
family photo's
scotch tape and scissors
red wrapping paper
a small cross, or a picture of Jesus
sheets of paper
favorite board games

The way to love anything is to realize that it might be lost.— G. K. Chesterton

SUNDAY—A Topic Introduction
Read I Corinthians 13:4-7 to your kids. Ask: "How do you know I love you? How do you know your sister/brother loves you?" Talk about loving each other.

MONDAY—A Simple Activity
Have the kids write a message to Dad—"I love you"—on a little circle of tissue or toilet paper, then tape the message onto the end of the tube so he can read it when he peers through the tube. Decorate or color the tube. A special Valentine!

TUESDAY—A Story Time
Read *The Velveteen Rabbit* to your children. Ask, and discuss: "What makes you feel loved?"

WEDNESDAY—A Self-esteem Builder

Get out your family photo's of your children when they were newborn babies. Tell them about their births and about what they were like as babies. Kids love to see old pictures of themselves and hear stories about their infancy.

THURSDAY—A Family Worship Time

Wrap a cross or picture of Jesus in gift wrap. Begin your evening by reading I Corinthians 13:4-7 aloud. Ask your kids: "Did you get any Valentines? Show them to us!" Read aloud all the messages of love printed on them. "Boy, you guys sure are loved! Can you tell us all the people who love you?" Have them list as many people as possible. "Do you know who loves you most? Who gave you the best Valentine's Day gift of love?" Have kids open the present and find Jesus.

Ask: "How can we love Jesus back?" Have each child create a Valentine for Jesus, writing on a red heart one way they can show they love Him.

FRIDAY—Another Simple Activity

Have a Valentine race. Mark start and finish lines and give each person two large, red paper hearts. When you say "GO!" kids must race by stepping only on their hearts—no feet can touch the carpet.

SATURDAY—A Special Event

Take a night out of your busy schedule to relax with your kids (with the television off). Play your favorite board games. We like Uno, Silly Beasts, Trouble, dominoes, Candy Land, Fish, and Chutes & Ladders.

RESOURCE SUGGESTION: *My Jesus Pocketbooks*, by Chariot Books, are full of inspirational thoughts that will make your child's day.

WEEK 8

Living Value for the Week: COMPASSION
Character: Jesus
Scripture: Luke 7:11-15
Memory Verse: *"When he saw the crowds, he had compassion on them, because they were harassed and helpless, like sheep without a shepherd."*— Matthew 9:36

Materials:
      paper bags
      crayons or markers
      straw
      a Kleenex
      a party blower
      a good kid's movie

Kindness influences more than eloquence.

SUNDAY—A Topic Introduction

Tell your kids how someone once was kind to you when you were in a tight spot. Tell how this made you feel.

MONDAY—A Simple Activity

If you have a pet at home, make a special time today to give it special care. Does the dog need bathing and grooming? Does the cat need a toy?

TUESDAY—A Story Time

Read the story of Jesus and the widow's son from Luke 7:11-17. Focus on verse 13: "When the Lord saw her, his heart went out to her . . .". Ask, and discuss: "When Jesus sees you, what is He concerned about?" Talk about any problems the kids mention that may need your—and the Lord's—understanding and help.

46

WEDNESDAY—A Self-esteem Builder

As you sit around the breakfast or dinner table, ask each person: "What is the nicest thing you've ever done for someone else?" Help the kids to feel like compassionate heroes.

THURSDAY—A Family Worship Time

Read Luke 7:11-17 from a good, dynamic translation such as *The Illustrated Bible*. Then give small paper bags to your children and ask them to create "paper bag puppets" of the characters in the story. (If you have many children, let each one make a Jesus, a widow, and a son.) They can use crayons or markers to draw the faces, and they can draw the garments or create them from construction paper. After their puppets are made, ask the kids to retell the story to you (they may want to do this several times).

FRIDAY—Another Simple Activity

Lie on the floor with a straw in your mouth and a Kleenex over the straw. Have your child sit beside your head, with a party blower ready. As you blow, the Kleenex will shoot up. Your child tries to catch the Kleenex in the roll of the party blower. Ask older kids: "How should we treat people when they 'blow it'—let us down?"

SATURDAY—A Special Event

Rent a good kid's movie that conveys a message of compassion. (We highly recommend Disney's "So Dear To My Heart.") After viewing the movie, take some time to talk to your kids about it. What happened in the story? What was the "point"? What did they learn?

RESOURCE SUGGESTION: *Cherry Cola Champions* (Chariot) is an excellent book for girls ages eight and older . It teaches the Living Value of godly compassion.

WEEK 9

Living Value for the Week: CONCERN (Loving the sick)
Character: Jesus
Scripture: Matthew 9:18-26
Memory Verse: *"Heal the sick who are there and tell them, 'The kingdom of God is near you.'"—Luke 10:9*

Materials: construction paper, scissors, and glue
               Play-Doh
               blank book or notebook with paper
               box (like an apple box from a grocery store)
               two or more tennis balls
               lots of shoes

The dew of compassion is a tear.—Lord Byron

SUNDAY—A Topic Introduction
Ask, and discuss: "Do you remember that time when you were sick? What helped you feel better? Who made you well?"

MONDAY—A Simple Activity
Hand out small (2"x6") slips of paper. Ask kids to write one prayer request on each, then loop them together to make a "prayer chain." Hang the prayer chain in a prominent spot and pray about the requests during the week. Put a star by names of friends or relatives who are sick.

TUESDAY—A Story Time
Read Matthew 9:18-26 to your kids. Act it out with them. Discuss: "What's easy and hard about being around sick people?"

WEDNESDAY—A Self-esteem Builder
Hand out pieces of Play-Doh and ask the children to make people."It's hard to make a person, isn't it? God must be very talented!" Now ask the kids to make ugly monsters with their Play-Doh.

48

"Does God love even these ugly monsters? Sure! He loves the ugly *and* the beautiful. Monsters aren't real, but God loves all people for what they are on the *inside*—whether they're pretty or not; whether they're sick or well."

THURSDAY—A Family Worship Time

First, practice your memory verse. Next, take a look at your prayer chain. Have some of your requests been answered yet? If so, take those links off. "Can you see how God is working? He is answering our prayers!"

Take your notebook or blank book and create a Family Prayer Book. Write down all of your family members' prayer requests, leaving space to mark the date when God has answered each prayer. Work together to dress up the cover of your prayer notebook and continued to pray together regularly for your requests this year. One family has done this for many years—and has seventeen *volumes* of answers!

FRIDAY—Another Simple Activity

Play "Box Bowling." Turn a box upside-down and cut three different-sized holes (shaped like the standard mouse hole in a base board, seen in cartoons) along one of the edges that will touch the floor. Place the box on the floor and take turns "bowling" your tennis balls at it. Sizes are worth 1-3-5 points. It's fun!

SATURDAY—A Special Event

Make a big pile of shoes in the center of your living room. When the lights go off, everyone races to put on a pair that match. Have a brief discussion about the special needs of someone you may know who is handicapped: not able to walk, not having a foot or leg, etc. Spend time in prayer for this person.

RESOURCE SUGGESTION: Little children enjoy William Coleman's books. Try *Today I Feel Like A Warm Fuzzy* (Bethany House).

WEEK 10

Living Value for the Week: CONCERN (Caring for others)
Character: Jesus
Scripture: Matthew 14:13-21
Memory Verse: *"Dear children, let us not love with words or tongue but with actions and in truth."* —I John 3:18

Materials: paper (for paper airplanes)
a bandana
"Secret Pal" cards (store bought or homemade)
some simple magic tricks
a ball of string
blank cards

Kindness is loving people more than they deserve.— Joseph Joubert

SUNDAY—A Topic Introduction
At the dinner table, Mom asks the smaller kids: "Why do I feed you?" Everyone help the kids respond to her question.

MONDAY—A Simple Activity
Read the account of Jesus feeding the five thousand in Matthew 14:13-21. Imagine how large a crowd five thousand people would be. Ask very young children to tell what they could buy with five thousand pennies.

TUESDAY—A Story Time
Sit in a circle. Holding a ball of string, begin an imaginary story in which your kids are the heroes in caring for someone. Part way into the story, toss the ball to another. Whoever gets it must continue the story. Repeat the process until all have had a chance to contribute.

WEDNESDAY—A Self-esteem Builder
To build up your children this week, have each person write

50

the name of a Secret Pal. Have each child think of something special he or she could do for the Secret Pal during the coming week: send an encouraging note, draw a picture, make a cookie, do something nice. Discuss: "Why do we feel good about ourselves when we help someone else?"

THURSDAY—A Family Worship Time

Read Matthew 14:13-21 to your children. "How did Jesus do that? Was He a magician?" Do a couple of simple magic tricks for your family. (You can buy a couple at a magic store, or better yet, get a magic book at your local library and practice up on "Glass Thru Table," "Disappearing Coin," "Bending Pencil," etc.)

If you pin a cracker-filled bandana under your coat, you'll be able to "magically" produce several crackers, one after another. "Is that a miracle? No. Jesus did *real* miracles and fed over five thousand people with just five loaves of bread and two fish. Why do you suppose He did that? Did He care about those people? Does He care for you? How do you know?"

FRIDAY—Another Simple Activity

Make paper airplanes. See who can throw their planes the farthest and who can land planes closest to a "landing target." Discuss: "Do you like to fly in airplanes? If your friend was afraid to fly, how could you show your concern for her and help her?"

SATURDAY—A Special Event

This weekend each child gets a "Date with Dad." Dad takes each child on a special outing for ice cream, a movie, a visit to a toy store, or whatever your kids would like to do.

PARENTING SUGGESTION: Let your kids know when you give money to the church, missions, or special ministry projects. They need to see your practical concern for others.

WEEK 11

Living Value for the Week: HELPFULNESS (Helping the lost)
Character: Jesus
Scripture: Matthew 18:12-14
Memory Verse: *"For the Son of Man came to seek and to save what was lost."—Luke 19:11*

Materials:
family photo albums
a stuffed toy sheep
pencils and paper
a compass, or a city street map
caramel corn, or some other fun snack

Nothing makes one feel so strong as a call for help.— George MacDonald

SUNDAY—A Topic Introduction
"Have you ever been lost?" Tell your kids about a time when you were lost. How did it happen? How did you get found again?

MONDAY—A Simple Activity
Take some time to look through your family photo albums. Remember any family members who have died or who live far away.

TUESDAY—A Story Time
Instead of reading, tell your kids, "I've lost my sheep! Can you help me find it?" After the kids find your previously hidden toy sheep, read Matthew 18:12-14 to them.

WEDNESDAY—A Self-esteem Builder
Have everyone draw an acrostic that tells about his or her

Secret Pal, revealing the pal's identity during dinner. Example:

        C - Creative
        O - Outstanding Artist
        L - Loving
        I - Intelligent
        N - Nice boy

THURSDAY—A Family Worship Time

First, teach the memory verse. Next, read Matthew 18:12-14. Explain to your children what a parable is—a story about nature or people that teaches us something about God. Ask each child: "If you were a sheep, what might cause you to get lost? Where would you get lost? What would the shepherd need to do for you to make you feel loved? How do you know that Jesus—the Good Shepherd—loves you right now?"

FRIDAY—Another Simple Activity

Take older kids to the woods in order to show them how to use a compass. (If you live in a big city, go downtown and explore ways to find the way home in an unfamiliar situation. Use a city street map.)

SATURDAY—A Special Event

Make a list of twenty silly activities ("stand on your head and hoot like an owl") and rare finds ("a magenta crayon"). Give a copy to your children and tell them to go on a scavenger hunt in the house and yard. State that the winner(s) will get served caramel corn by the runner-ups. While eating, talk about losing and finding as it relates to personal salvation.

RESOURCE SUGGESTION: Our family has enjoyed reading C. S. Lewis' great series, *The Chronicles of Narnia.*

WEEK 12

Living Value for the Week: HELPFULNESS
Character: Hur
Scripture: Exodus 17:8-13
Memory Verse: *"Carry each other's burdens, and in this way you will fulfill the law of Christ."—Galatians 6:2*

Materials: a Lifesaver
              string
              paper
              safety pins
              marking pens
              a shoe box

Ten rules for getting rid of the blues: Go out and do something for someone else, and repeat it nine times.

SUNDAY—A Topic Introduction
Have your kids help Mom or Dad make dinner. Choose something simple like: macaroni and cheese, frozen vegetables, and quick rolls.

MONDAY—A Simple Activity
Tie a Lifesaver candy in the center of a long piece of string. Put the ends of the string in the mouths of two kids. Have them race to see who can get to the candy without using their hands. Ask: "When was the last time you appreciated a pair of hands that helped you? When have you helped someone else? What was that like?"

TUESDAY—A Story Time

Have a contest to see how long kids can hold something (like a book or a shoe) with arms outstretched from their sides. As they are straining to hold on, tell the story of Moses on the mountain with Aaron and Hur.

WEDNESDAY—A Self-esteem Builder

Make up small buttons that say, "I'm a Helper!" Look for reasons to pin them on your kids today.

THURSDAY—A Family Worship Time

Read aloud Exodus 17:8-13. Talk about Hur's small act of helpfulness and how it made such a big difference.

Remind your kids of all the helpful things they have done during the week. As your way of saying thanks, introduce "Bible Charades," a fun game where one person or team, without saying a word, acts out a story from the Bible. We find it best to finish the skit before the other team gets to guess what the story was.

FRIDAY—Another Simple Activity

Play family bingo. Use pieces of paper, folded over four times, to produce sixteen squares. Each person in turn names a favorite thing, all write it somewhere on their sheets until all sixteen squares are filled. Then Dad reads his list, left to right, until someone matches four in a row.

SATURDAY—A Special Event

Get the children involved in decorating a shoe box. Then distribute slips of paper and ask everyone to write down ideas for helping people. Maybe a neighbor needs weeding done, or Grandma needs help cleaning her garage. Put the slips in the box and mix them up. Pull out a "help slip" and have the family join together to accomplish the task today. Place the box on a shelf and use it occasionally.

RESOURCE SUGGESTION: For teaching young children the value of helpfulness, try Chariot's animal pop-up book, *Joshua Lends a Hand.*

WEEK 13

Living Value for the Week: HOLINESS
Special Celebration Days (optional): Passion Week
Character: Jesus
Scriptures: Various events in Jesus' life
Memory Verse: *"We have been made holy through the sacrifice of the body of Jesus Christ once for all."*—Hebrews 10:10

Materials:
    pillows
    unleavened bread (crackers)
    grape juice
    pencils and paper
    thank-you notes

This is the very perfection of a man, to find out his own imperfections.— Augustine

SUNDAY—A Topic Introduction

Ask younger children to draw a "perfect" circle for you. Then show them how to do it by using the bottom of a jar or glass. Discuss: "How close did you come to being 'just perfect'?"

MONDAY—A Simple Activity

Read Matthew 21:12-17, about Jesus in the temple . . . then have a pillow fight!

TUESDAY—A Story Time

Read Matthew 13:33. "What do you think Jesus' story means?" As you talk about the meaning of the yeast—the holy lives of Christians in the Kingdom—why not make some bread together?

WEDNESDAY—A Self-esteem Builder

This was the night Jesus ate the last supper with His disciples. Read Matthew 26:17-30 and have communion at home with your family. Serve grape juice and crackers to relive Jesus' last meal. "Jesus sure loved us . . . so much that He died for us, as a perfect, holy sacrifice."

THURSDAY—A Family Worship Time

Read Luke 22:47-53. If possible, go outside to a garden and read this account. Tell your kids the story of the events leading up to Jesus' arrest. Make these points:

  A. Jesus was God's Son.
  B. God sent Him to show us how to live.
  C. He never sinned (He was perfectly holy).
  D. People rejected Him.
  E. He died willingly for us.

Have a time of prayer, thanking Jesus for loving us so much.

FRIDAY—Another Simple Activity

On this Good Friday, read John 19:17-30. Ask your kids if they would like to write a thank-you note to Jesus for what He did for them on the cross. Suggest that they include their notes in an envelope with their offerings on Easter morning.

SATURDAY—A Special Event

Read Luke 23:50-56. As a way to remember the day Christ's body lay in the tomb, spend a quiet morning or afternoon together: walking in the woods, strolling through a park, visiting a cemetery, or visiting another, special, quiet place.

RESOURCE SUGGESTION: Here's an excellent book for parents: Andrew Murray's *How to Raise Your Children for Christ*.

WEEK 14

Living Values for the Week: FAITH and WORSHIP (Because of the resurrection)
Special Celebration Day (optional): Easter
Character: Jesus
Scripture: Luke 24; John 20; Matthew 28
Memory Verse: *"He is not here; he has risen!"—Luke 24:6a*

Materials: flannel and flannelgraph characters (borrow from a Sunday School teacher?)
paper and marking pens
old magazines
scissors
glue
a birthday cake

If Christ has not been raised, our preaching is useless and so is your faith.
—The Apostle Paul

SUNDAY—A Topic Introduction
Rush into the kids rooms and say: "Wake up! Jesus is alive! Wake up!" Talk about how *good* the Good News really was the first time it was proclaimed.

MONDAY—A Simple Activity
Jesus was in the tomb for three days and then He reappeared. Celebrate by playing hide and seek. Discuss: "How do we know Jesus isn't still hidden?"

TUESDAY—A Story Time
Read the story of Jesus' resurrection from Luke 24. Follow-up by having Mom or Dad talk about a time of meeting some-one again after many years of being apart. Ask kids to tell how

58

that experience would be like and unlike meeting Jesus after the Resurrection.

WEDNESDAY—A Self-esteem Builder

First, draw each other's names from a hat. Then give each person a big sheet of paper with the words "Jesus Loves You" printed on it. Each person is to use crayons and pictures cut from old magazines to create a collage of the person whose name was drawn. Present the works of art to each other, explaining how they tell something good about the person's personality.

THURSDAY—A Family Worship Time

Read the story of Jesus' resurrection from John 20. Ask each child what character they would like to make, then give them some flannel, markers, scissors, and glue to create the various flannelgraph characters to tell the story of the resurrection. You may wish to display some flannelgraph characters from your Sunday School class to demonstrate to the kids what their characters will look like. After the characters are all made, ask one of your children to use them to tell the resurrection story.

Get kids' ideas: "What would be a good way to worship Jesus tonight for rising from the dead?"

FRIDAY—Another Simple Activity

Turn your memory verse into a code and let your kids try to decode it. (An easy way to make a code would be to move each letter over two places: "A" becomes "C"; "B" becomes "D"; etc. So "Jg jcu tkugp" is "He has risen.")

SATURDAY—A Special Event

After lunch, remind the kids that each of us not only has a real birthday but a "spiritual birthday" (the day we first loved Jesus). What better time to celebrate kids' spiritual birthdays than during the Easter season? Have them help mix, bake, and decorate their cakes (and eat them, too!).

WEEK 15

Living Value for the Week: FORGIVENESS (Rather than revenge)
Character: Moses
Scripture: Exodus 2
Memory Verse: *"If someone strikes you on one cheek, turn to him the other also."—Luke 6:29a*

Materials: aluminum foil
three pop bottles
paper and markers
Scotch tape, stapler, index cards
hot-fudge sundaes
Nerf basketball

The best manner of "avenging" ourselves is by not resembling him who has injured us.— Jane Porter

SUNDAY—A Topic Introduction
"What does the word 'revenge' mean?" Have one of your children look up the definition in a dictionary and then discuss it together.

MONDAY—A Simple Activity
Twist two inches of aluminum foil into a ring. Put three pop bottles in a line, spaced one foot apart. Mark a start line and have kids try to toss the ring onto bottle necks. The nearest bottle is worth 1 point; the middle, 3 points; the farthest, 5 points. Discuss: "Some things are easier to do than others. Why is it easier to hit someone back than it is to keep from hitting back?"

TUESDAY—A Story Time
Get kids involved in a wrestling match with Dad on the carpet. Dad is given various handicaps, depending on the size of the kids (he can't use arms or legs; he must keep hands closed, etc.). Then tell the story of Moses killing the Egyptian, from Exodus 2.

WEDNESDAY—A Self-esteem Builder

Draw names. Each person is to draw a house for the one whose name he or she got, making the house as that person would like it. The house should be arranged and decorated in a way that will say something about the person for whom it is designed. Share your designs with each other and talk about them (from Wayne Rickerson's *Family Fun Times*).

THURSDAY—A Family Worship Time

Talk about Moses and the consequences of his vengeful attitude. Instead of being patient, Moses sought revenge . . . and it cost him everything he had. Get out your Nerf basketball and have a quick game, but have one person pretend to be a mean player. "How do you want to treat to this 'meany'?" Talk about alternative responses. What does taking revenge accomplish? How does patience and forgiveness help? What did Jesus say to do? (see the memory verse).

FRIDAY—Another Simple Activity

Practice saying the memory verse. Then tell kids: "Since we don't hit in our family, we can't practice doing this verse tonight. So let's replace the word 'strikes' with 'kiss' (or 'hug'). How would that work? Now we can practice!"

SATURDAY—A Special Event

On index cards, write Bible verses that refer to objects you can find around your home (for example, see Prov. 11:1; Psa. 1:3; Prov. 15:17; Matt. 6:6; Prov. 27:9, etc.). Hide the cards around your home for a scavenger hunt, each a clue to the next object (for example, the clue about a tree is located with the vegetables, and the vegetable clue is under the perfume). Hand kids the first clue and let them start the hunt. At the end, celebrate with hot-fudge sundaes. While eating, discuss: "Has anybody wanted to 'hit back' this week? What happened?"

RESOURCE SUGGESTION: We love "The Donut Man" music tapes.

WEEK 16

Living Value for the Week: PATIENCE
Character: Moses
Scripture: Exodus 2 and 3
Memory Verse: *"Be patient, then, brothers, until the Lord's coming."—James 5:7a*

Materials: water colors
paper
marbles
ice cubes
a big pan

They also serve who only stand and wait.— John Milton

SUNDAY—A Topic Introduction

Ask your kids: "What things are you waiting for?" Pray with your kids about their responses, and then tell them: "This week we're going to talk about being patient."

MONDAY—A Simple Activity

Set up a simple, outdoor obstacle course (go under a chair, over the dog's house, etc.) for younger kids. See if everyone can get through it under two minutes. Ask: "How old would you have to be to do this in less than a minute? Why is it hard to wait until you're a 'big kid'?"

TUESDAY—A Story Time

Have smaller kids try to sit still for a few minutes while just watching the family pet (the pet may be sleeping). Then tell them the story of Moses as a shepherd, from Exodus 2 and 3. Talk about what Moses' life must have been like.

WEDNESDAY—A Self-esteem Builder

With your paints and paper, draw a picture of someone else in the family doing something nice.

THURSDAY—A Family Worship Time

After reviewing your memory verse, ask everyone, "When do you find it hard to be patient?" Parents share their answers first.

Retell the story of Moses and the Egyptian. Hand out slips of paper and ask each person to write down one situation in which they need more patience (jot younger kids' responses for them). Pass the slips around and have everyone pray for someone else in the family.

FRIDAY—Another Simple Activity

Fill a pan with crushed ice and put a dozen marbles in the bottom. Two people try to take the marbles out with their toes without spilling any ice or water. (It's nippy but fun!) Discuss: "We can't stand keeping our feet in the ice! What else can't you stand?"

SATURDAY—A Special Event

Kids get to have a date with Mom. It's Mom's turn to plan on taking each child on a one-on-one date wherever they would like to go (within reason, of course). Tonight, schedule the dates on your family calendar. (Note: 99% of the girls will want Mom to take them shopping. Remind them that the focus of your conversation will be: patience!)

RESOURCE SUGGESTION: Your children can learn the value of patience by reading *Old Ruff and the Mother Bird* (for ages 3-8, by Chariot).

WEEK 17

Living Value for the Week: COURAGE
Character: Moses
Scripture: Exodus 7—12
Memory Verse: *"The Lord himself goes before you and will be with you . . . Do not be afraid."—Deuteronomy 31:8*

Materials: a tape recorder (or video camcorder)
                crayons
                paper

"A ship in harbor is safe, but that is not what ships are for."—John A. Shedd

SUNDAY—A Topic Introduction

Tell your kids about a time when you were afraid, but you did something that took courage.

MONDAY—A Simple Activity

Play tag. One person is "it" and chases the rest. You are safe (cannot be tagged for a count of 3) when you lie on your back with your feet in the air. Great fun! Later, ask: "Have you ever wanted to just 'lie down' instead of doing something scary that needed doing? What did you do?"

TUESDAY—A Story Time

Tell your kids the story of Moses and Pharaoh, from Exodus 7-12.

WEDNESDAY—A Self-esteem Builder

Each person selects objects in the house that remind him or her of a quality in another member of the family. (For example, I'd pick a quilt for Patti, because it reminds me of her creativity.) Share your objects and your mutual appreciation with each other.

THURSDAY—A Family Worship Time

Start by retelling the story of Moses and Pharaoh. Divide up the parts in the story (as few as two: Moses and Pharaoh; or as many as eight, with Aaron, God, the crowd, etc.) and make a taped dramatic production of the story. Make sure to include not just dialogue but the sound of frogs croaking, the thunder of a hailstorm, the buzzing of flies, etc. After your production is completed, enjoy a snack while listening to/viewing your radio/video drama.

FRIDAY—Another Simple Activity

Everyone draw a picture in answer to: "How do I feel when I lose a game? When I'm home alone? When everyone is arguing?" Focus on the feelings that come through in the pictures. (It's best to draw feeling pictures with the opposite hand—left hand for right-handers.) Discuss what kinds of courage it takes to "survive" those kinds of situations.

SATURDAY—A Special Event

Experience your own family "exodus." Turn off the lights and whisper to the kids to bring one secret "treasure" along on a special trip. Sneak out of your houses, silently drive for a treat, and have everyone in the car share what they brought along, and why. Ask: "What must it have been like for the Israelites to sneak away from their homes at night? What would have been joyful? What would have been sad?"

RESOURCE SUGGESTION: Chariot Books has published a series for boys (8-12), *Sports Stories for Boys*, teaching the valuses of courage, confidence, and cooperation.

WEEK 18

Living Value for the Week: PERSEVERANCE (Without complaining)
Character: Moses
Scripture: Exodus 14; Numbers 11, 20, 21
Memory Verse: *"Let us not become weary in doing good, for at the proper time we will reap a harvest if we do not give up."—Galatians 6:9*

Materials: paper and pencils
               old magazines
               scissors and glue
               an old pair of glasses
               glitter

The difference between perseverance and obstinacy is that one often comes from a strong will and the other from a strong won't.— Henry Ward Beecher

SUNDAY—A Topic Introduction
Say: "Tell me about the best day you've ever had. Did it seem long or short?"

MONDAY—A Simple Activity
Ask your kids to list all of the complaints and excuses Moses gave God as you read through Exodus 3 and 4. Then ask: "What are the worst excuses you've ever heard?"

TUESDAY—A Story Time
Read various "complaint" stories in Exodus 14 and Numbers 11, 20, 21. Ask: "How do you like it when somebody is always complaining?"

66

WEDNESDAY—A Self-esteem Builder

Have everyone in the family write each other a letter of appreciation this week. You may need to help your kids focus on "what makes this person special." Give the letters to each other and read them aloud after you've gathered in a circle.

THURSDAY—A Family Worship Time

Take an old pair of glasses and have the kids fancy them up with glitter and sparkles. Ask if anyone is struggling with a school or a friendship problem, and have the "complainer" put on the world-famous Glory Glasses! (Guaranteed to make the wearer see things in a new light, the Glory Glasses call for the wearer to talk about the positive things in the situation and the ways God may be working in that situation.) Pray together for perseverance.

FRIDAY—Another Simple Activity

Wayne Rickerson offers a great way to study grumbling: Wait for kids to ask: "What's for lunch?" Take the kids on a mealtime campout to a bedroom, where they'll find manna (cookies) and quail (beef jerky). Have everyone thank God for His provision.

SATURDAY—A Special Event

Take out that family scrapbook you began earlier in the year. Have everyone go through recent photographs, awards, cards, or anything else that should be added, and bring your scrapbook up to date.

RESOURCE SUGGESTION: Try *Adam Raccoon and the Race to Victory Mountain* (Chariot) to teach your young child the value of perseverance .

WEEK 19

Living Value for the Week: PEACEFULNESS
Character: Moses
Scripture: Numbers 16
Memory Verse: *"And the peace of God, which transcends all understanding, will guard your hearts and your minds in Christ Jesus."—Matthew 6:20*

Materials: puppets (any kind will do)
              newspapers and magazine advertisements
              glue and scissors
              magazines
              pencils, and a long sheet of paper

Contentment is natural wealth; luxury is artificial poverty.—Socrates

SUNDAY—A Topic Introduction
Ask, and discuss: "If you had a thousand dollars, how would you spend it? And if you had to spend it on others, how would you do so?"

MONDAY—A Simple Activity
Ask the kids what their favorite family game has been so far (my guess? box bowling!) and play it with them.

TUESDAY—A Story Time
Tell the events of Numbers 16. It is a bit complex, so you might use some puppets to help. Focus on the discontentment of the people. Ask kids to tell about how they react to situations that make them nervous.

WEDNESDAY—A Self-esteem Builder

Take out the puppets you used yesterday and give them to your kids. Ask them to tell a story about themselves. (Or, if they are too young to grasp that, you use the puppets to tell a story about your kids doing something that helped them be content.)

THURSDAY—A Family Worship Time

Chat with your family about all of the stories you have studied during the past several weeks, as you've looked at the life of Moses. Take a long sheet of paper and help your family create a frieze, or mural, of the life of Moses. Using crayons to draw, pictures or words cut from magazines, posed photo's, or anything else you deem useful, create a story-board that depicts various events in Moses' life.

FRIDAY—Another Simple Activity

Sit in a circle and have one person jump into the center of the circle. Go around and have everyone make predictions about: "Where (name) will be in fifteen years." Let everybody have a turn, then discuss: "What kind of life would be the most peaceful for me?"

SATURDAY—A Special Event

Take your family window shopping at the mall. In the car, discuss all the things you'd like to have some day. After you get home, get out newspaper advertisements and cut out some of the items you've talked about. Make a poster. On one side, glue all the things that will last; on the other side, glue the things that won't last. Talk about the satisfaction of permanent things.

RESOURCE SUGGESTION: The book *Stories from the Growing Years* (Chariot) teaches the value of peacefulness and contentment for kids age eight and up. It is just one of many good books in the *Grandma's Attic* series.

WEEK 20

Living Value for the Week: PRAYERFULNESS (Of a biblical mother)
Special Celebration Day (optional): Mother's Day
Character: Hannah
Scripture: I Samuel 1
Memory Verse: *"Pray continually; give thanks in all circumstances."—I Thessalonians 5:17, 18a*

Materials: crayons
                construction paper
                decorations
                paper and pencils

"Fathers, build into your children the greatness of their mothers.
—Chuck Swindoll

SUNDAY—A Topic Introduction
Dad, help the kids to get up early, cook Mom breakfast, decorate her chair like a "throne," and offer her reasons why they appreciate her.

MONDAY—A Simple Activity
Dad, help the children create special hand-made cards for Mom that are crayoned or painted (or: they could create a certificate of appreciation).

TUESDAY—A Story Time
Read the story of Hannah praying for a child, and of God answering her prayers. Talk about what is "different" about a prayerful person. How does such a person make decisions?

WEDNESDAY—A Self-esteem Builder

Take up a paper and pencil. Ask: "What three words best describe Mom? What three words do you wish best described *you?*" (Help your kids focus on behavior words rather than merely appearance words.)

THURSDAY—A Family Worship Time

Dad, it is your responsibility to see that Mom has a night off. So set the table and get the kids helping you prepare dinner. My suggestion: a simple, six-course meal—

1. Appetizer (crackers and cream cheese)
2. Tossed green salad
3. Clear soup
4. Small portion of meat and vegetable (roast chicken leg, or pork chop)
5. Fruit (an apple)
6. Dessert (ice cream)

At some point during the meal, ask Mom to share about ways that her children are an answer to prayer for her.

FRIDAY—Another Simple Activity

After breakfast, gather in a circle for a time of sentence prayers. First ask everyone to share about one thing they are worried about or thankful for as they start a new day.

SATURDAY—A Special Event

Mom probably has little energy left by Saturday, so give her "time off" while the kids join Dad in doing those awful jobs Mom hates to face (like scrubbing floors, windows, and bathrooms).

PARENTING SUGGESTION: If you're a single parent, have your oldest child coordinate some of these activities for you. It will make him or her feel grown up!

WEEK 21

Living Value for the Week: OBEDIENCE
Characters: Adam and Eve
Scripture: Genesis 3
Memory Verse: *"Children, obey your parents in the Lord, for this is right."—Ephesians 6:1*

Materials: paper and pencils
a Bible dictionary
a Bible atlas or other resource book

The potential possibilities of any child are the most intriguing and stimulating in all creation.— Ray L. Wilbur

SUNDAY—A Topic Introduction

Ask, and discuss: "How do I show you that I love you? How do *you* show *me*? How does God show us He loves us? How do we show God we love Him?"

MONDAY—A Simple Activity

Play a different version of "Simon Says." Reverse the rules: Kids must do only what "Mom/Dad says." Simon can be ignored!

TUESDAY—A Story Time

If at all possible, go outside and tell your children the story of Adam and Eve in the garden of Eden. Discuss: "Why do you think Adam and Eve didn't obey God?"

WEDNESDAY—A Self-esteem Builder

Everyone sit in a circle. One person gets into the center. Each family member, in turn, tells about a way that person has been known to be obedient in the last month. Be positive!

THURSDAY—A Family Worship Time

Ask your kids to tell you the story of Adam and Eve in the garden. They disobeyed God and it hurt them very much. "Do you know how we can show God that we love Him? Read I John 5:3 for the answer."

Talk for a few minutes about how obedience is the proof of love for God. Next, hold a family auction. Begin by showing your kids a short list of prizes (a date with Dad; the right to choose one night's dinner; a night at the movies; a trip to the zoo; any special privileges you can think up). Your kids will bid five-minute time slots helping Mom or Dad around the house. Auction prizes to the highest bidder. They collect after they've "paid" their time in work.

FRIDAY—Another Simple Activity

Play "Twenty Questions." Think of a person, place, or thing. Your kids ask you twenty "yes" or "no" questions, then they have to guess what you're thinking. Ask kids if they think it is possible to know what a parent wants them to do *before* being told to do it?

SATURDAY—A Special Event

Have a special "preparing for Sunday" time. Find out the pastor's Sunday sermon text and have your children read it aloud. Look up background information in a Bible dictionary; talk about the history, people, places, or events in the passage. Try to figure out the point of the passage, and then brainstorm with older children: "What is there in this passage that calls us to obedience?"

WEEK 22

Living Value for the Week: INITIATIVE (Obeying even when it means hard work)
Character: Noah
Scripture: Genesis 6—8
Memory Verse: *"This is love for God: to obey his commands. And his commands are not burdensome."—I John 5:3*

Materials:
    paper and markers
    stuffed animals
    pillows and cushions
    fabric crayons
    white muslin or cotton fabric
    Play-Doh
    an iron
    a white dinner plate
    permanent markers

Sloth, like rust, consumes faster than labor wears, while the used key is always bright.— Benjamin Franklin

SUNDAY—A Topic Introduction
Show kids a picture of a ship at sea. Ask: "How easy or hard would it be to build a huge boat? What steps would you need to take? What tools would you use? How long would you have to work?"

MONDAY—A Simple Activity
Using fabric crayons, have the kids draw pictures of Noah and the ark. Iron them onto muslin.

TUESDAY—A Story Time
Don't just tell the story from Genesis 6—8 . . . build an ark out of sofa cushions, pillows, and blankets, fill it with stuffed animals,

74

and pretend you are Noah's family! Then, tell the story.

WEDNESDAY—A Self-esteem Builder

With permanent markers, write on a white plate, "You Are Special!" Let this be a special "reward" plate for the next few weeks. Anyone doing an outstanding job of obeying his or her parents will be awarded the place of honor and will eat off this grand plate. Give special praise when kids take the initiative to do something *before* you ask.

THURSDAY—A Family Worship Time

Bring out the fabric "Noah" pictures your kids made on Monday night. Get out some coordinating material, needles, and thread and have your kids help you sew a fringe fabric onto their pictures (even the young ones can be of some help while you sew). If you use 8x10-inch rectangles, these fabric pictures can make nice gifts as pillows, quilts, or wall hangings. A frilly edge adds a nice touch. As you sew, be sure to offer your children plenty of warm encouragement about their work. And talk with them: "Do you think it was hard for Noah to obey? Why? Do you keep working even when it's hard?"

FRIDAY—Another Simple Activity

Give your kids Play-Doh and ask them to build an ark—complete with their "favorite" animals. Ask: "What would have been the most exciting thing for Noah when he obeyed God? What would have been the hardest thing for him to do?"

SATURDAY—A Special Event

After a week spent focusing on Noah, take an all-day trip to the zoo. Remind the kids that God saved two (and sometimes eight) of each animal through Noah's obedience.

RESOURCE SUGGESTION: Tim LaHaye's *How To Study the Bible for Yourself* (Harvest House) is an excellent family resource for learning and teaching personal Bible study methods.

WEEK 23

Living Value for the Week: TRUST (Obeying even in uncertainty)
Character: Joshua
Scripture: Joshua 6
Memory Verse: *"Trust in the Lord with all your heart and lean not on your own understanding."—Proverbs 3:5*

Materials: pillows
                  rubber gloves
                  milk
                  wrapping paper
                  pen and paper

How calmly may we commit ourselves to the hands of Him who bears up the world.— Jean Paul Richter

SUNDAY—A Topic Introduction
Ask your kids: "Have you ever been asked to obey . . . without knowing *why?* Why is it so hard to do?"

MONDAY—A Simple Activity
Go outside and play freeze tag with your kids: "It" tries to freeze the others; others try to free those frozen. Later, ask: "Have you ever been so afraid that you 'froze up'? What happened?"

TUESDAY—A Story Time
Walk around your house seven times with your children. Tell them to look very closely to notice anything that might need repairing, things that might eventually weaken the structure. (If they can't find anything—great; talk about how strong your house is.) Then read your children the story of Jericho's tumbling walls, from Joshua 6.

76

WEDNESDAY—A Self-esteem Builder

Take a moment to "bless" each of your children. Place your hands on their heads, one at a time, and say: "I'm so proud of you, son/daughter. The reason is . . .". Talk about how God's blessing is on all those who love and obey Him—even in uncertainty.

THURSDAY—A Family Worship Time

Tell a story about a time when you had to obey someone, even though you did not know the reasons for what you were told to do. Ask your kids, "Why is it good to learn to obey?" Listen to their answers. Point out that Joshua had to obey some "silly-sounding" commands of God, but his obedience led to the capture of Jericho.

Retell the story of Joshua 6, but use pillows and cushions to build the city "walls." Then have the family march around them, blow imaginary trumpets, shout, and tear those walls down—by jumping on them (the very young kids will want to do this several times). Close with prayer for greater trust in God.

FRIDAY—Another Simple Activity

Ever tried glove milking? Fill a rubber glove with milk, put pin holes in the fingers, and have the kids see who can "milk" the most in a minute. (Note: This is lots of fun but it can get messy!) Ask: "What special kinds of trust do farmers have to have?" (They have to trust God for rain, sunshine, healthy animals, etc.)

SATURDAY—A Special Event

Decorate your dining room with streamers and a sign reading "Happy Kids Day!" Serve pizza and shakes, and give each child a big hug for past trust in the goodness of parents and of God.

RESOURCE SUGGESTION: Chariot's *Critter County* board books offer children, ages one to three, a great way to develop the Living Value of trust. Each book tells children of a time during the day in which God is with them.

WEEK 24

Living Value for the Week: DEDICATION (Obeying even if I don't want to)
Character: Jonah
Scripture: Jonah
Memory Verse: *"Endure hardship as discipline; God is treating you as sons."*—Hebrews 12:7a

Materials:
  rose petals
  netting or loosely-woven material
  fish-shaped crackers
  string
  magazines
  scissors
  glue
  big sheets of paper
  bicycles

Every noble work is at first impossible.— Thomas Carlyle

SUNDAY—A Topic Introduction

Everybody answer this question: "Tell about something you were 'supposed to' do, but you didn't want to do it. Did you do it? Why? Why not?"

MONDAY—A Simple Activity

Have each of your kids gather a small handful of rose petals (the old, dry petals are best). Put them in a square of netting, tie the netting up with string to create a sachet and use or give away. Talk about rose bushes: What's 'sweet' about them? (the flowers). What's hurtful about them? (the thorns on their stems). How is obeying like a rose bush?"

78

TUESDAY—A Story Time

Tell your children the story of Jonah and the fish. Serve fish-shaped crackers for a snack as they listen.

WEDNESDAY—A Self-esteem Builder

Give each child a big sheet of paper (about 12"x24"). Spread magazines on your dining room table, along with scissors and glue. Ask each child to create a "personal collage" using pictures, words, and symbols that represent their likes, abilities, favorite places, people and things. Allow plenty of time for this. Hang the collages in a prominent place for at least a week.

THURSDAY—A Family Worship Time

Begin by retelling the story of Jonah, then give everyone several parts (Jonah, God, sailor, Ninevans, the huge fish) and act out the story of Jonah being called by God, running away, being tossed into the sea and swallowed, and finally preaching in Ninevah.

Next, ask your children to draw pictures of the part they liked best. As they color, talk about obeying even when it is difficult. Ask if they can think of something God wants them to do. You may have to suggest ideas, like inviting a friend to church or being kind to someone. Ask them to decide what God wants them to do, then pray about it together.

FRIDAY—Another Simple Activity

Have a fish dinner, using one large fish only. Invite kids to help you buy it and prepare it. At supper, talk about which is better: Eating a fish—or being eaten by one?

SATURDAY—A Special Event

Go fishing at a local lake or river. Plan ahead to get all prepared: buy or borrow poles, get bait, find a good place, etc.

RESOURCE SUGGESTION: For great family devotional ideas, read Carolyn Wiliford's *Devotions for Families that Can't Sit Still* (Victor Books).

WEEK 25

Living Value for the Week: RESOURCEFULNESS (By helping fathers and others)
Special Celebration Day (optional): Father's Day
Characters: Mordecai & Esther
Scripture: Esther
Memory Verse: *"I can do everything through him who gives me strength."—Philippians 4:13*

Materials: paper and pencils
                  ribbon
                  candle and matches
                  aluminum foil

When you influence a child, you have changed a life. When you influence a father, you have changed a family.—Bobb Biehl

SUNDAY—A Topic Introduction
Dad, take some time to tell your children about your father and grandfather. Be sure to include a story about the times you felt closest to your father.

MONDAY—A Simple Activity
Cut out little paper hammers, saws, and wrenches. Have kids write one idea for helping Dad on each tool (wash car, sweep garage, etc.). Present a "toolbox" to Dad at dinner.

TUESDAY—A Story Time
Tell the story of Esther, how she honored God and her stepfather, Mordecai, by bravely and resourcefully helping her people.

WEDNESDAY—A Self-esteem Builder

It means much to children when their father pays special attention to them. Dad, make an "Esther Award" out of paper and ribbon, then look for an appropriate time to award it to your son or daughter. The award is given for honoring Dad (helping him, obeying him, showing special respect, or coming up with a good idea).

THURSDAY—A Family Worship Time

Before beginning, Dad will need to sit down for several minutes and write out a "blessing" to each child. A blessing is a letter that describes the child's qualities (*not* his or her talents) and envisions a great future for him or her. For example, my letter encouraged my son's creativity, sensitivity, and sense of humor, then briefly envisioned him helping people as he walked with God.

Light a candle and sit around your dining table. Explain what a blessing is, then Dad places his hand on the child's shoulders and reads his blessing. Close with a prayer of thanksgiving.

FRIDAY—Another Simple Activity

Twist aluminum foil into a king's scepter and play "Red Light/Green Light" or "Simon Says" (but change it to "The King Says").

SATURDAY—A Special Event

Get out pencils and a large sheet of paper and draw your family ancestry. Don't just write names, jot down facts about each person, tell stories or look at photo's. Go back as far as you can. Help your children see their family heritage.

PARENTING SUGGESTION: More dads need encouragement and assistance than need criticism! Find a friend or relative who is also a dad. Share some friendly encouragement or advice about parenting.

81

WEEK 26

Living Value for the Week: LOYALTY (To our mates)
Special Celebration Day (optional): Wedding Anniversary
Character: Moses and Israel
Scripture: Leviticus 23
Memory Verse: *"Submit to one another out of reverence for Christ."—Ephesians 5:21*

Materials: wedding photo's
               books on the meanings of names
               index cards, pens, and paper
               dice and buttons

Loyalty means nothing unless it has at its heart the absolute principle of self-sacrifice.— Woodrow Wilson

SUNDAY—A Topic Introduction
Get out your wedding pictures and tell the children about your wedding. Ask: "Do you know what promises Mom and Dad made to each other at the wedding?"

MONDAY—A Simple Activity
For a fun outside game, try "hang tag." It's like any other tag, but you are "safe" whenever you are hanging from something, and your feet don't touch the ground. Later, discuss: "Has anybody ever 'left you hanging' when you were depending on them? What happened?"

TUESDAY—A Story Time
Read Leviticus 23 to your kids and explain that God wants us to remember important events and to celebrate them. Discuss: "What are some events that our family remembers and celebrates each year?"

WEDNESDAY—A Self-esteem Builder
At your local library, find books that explain the meanings of

82

names (try *The Best Baby Name Book Ever* or some other baby-naming book). Ask your child to research his name. Write it, along with a description and an appropriate verse, on a decorative piece of paper. Display this name-plate on your refrigerator.

THURSDAY—A Family Worship Time

On index cards, write questions about your wedding and marriage. (Examples: Where did we go on our first date? What did I say when I asked Mom to marry me? Where was our first home? What was Mom's nickname for Dad? Create your own questions; (make sure some of them are funny!) Sit around your living room and look at old pictures of Mom and Dad. Then pass out the cards and give a "pop quiz" on this subject. Finish the quiz by asking, "How do Mom and Dad show that they love and are loyal to each other?"

FRIDAY—Another Simple Activity

Take a nature walk in the woods or in a park. Talk about trees having roots that keep them in place. Discuss: "What roots—family history and traditions—help our family 'stay in place'?"

SATURDAY—A Special Event

Play "The Family Game" together. Draw a house on a large sheet of paper, with fifty numbered squares inside it. Create a series of cards that ask questions (for example: What is your favorite family memory? What three words describe you? If you had $100, what would you buy? Can you say Ephesians 5:21?, etc.) Play this like you'd play most simple board games: Everyone has a game piece (a button), each person rolls the dice to answer one question and advance the rolled number of squares. The first person to get to the end of the fifty squares wins. Consider adding some "action squares" to the game—if you land on one you have to cartwheel, meow, or do some other silly activity.

RESOURCE SUGGESTION: If you have a blended family as a result of prior marriages, consider the book *My Parents Got a Divorce* (Chariot), for kids age eight to fifteen.

WEEK 27

Living Value for the Week: HELPFULNESS (Toward missionary friends)
Character: Paul
Scripture: Acts 13, 14, 16
Memory Verse: *"It is more blessed to give than to receive."—Acts 20:35b*

Materials: missionary letters
      paper, pencils, and crayons
      large sheet of butcher paper
      stationery and envelopes
      encyclopedia or atlas
      a globe
      small gifts
      a picnic basket

As the purse is emptied, the heart is filled.— Victor Hugo

SUNDAY—A Topic Introduction

Select a missionary family that your family can learn about. Introduce them to your children by reading their prayer cards or letters.

MONDAY—A Simple Activity

Using a globe or atlas, have your kids locate the missionary family, then suggest ways your family could assist them.

TUESDAY—A Story Time

For your story time, read excerpts of Paul's missionary journeys, from Acts 13, 14, 16 (or read about Paul's travels from a Bible story book). Talk about the "farthest from home" each member of the family has ever been. Ask children to suggest the special needs of those who are away from home.

WEDNESDAY—A Self-esteem Builder

Have your child lie down on butcher paper and trace around him or her with a crayon. Next, instruct your child to fill in his or her outline by coloring in all of the details. Children could add clothes, jewelry, or anything they'd like.

THURSDAY—A Family Worship Time

Before you begin, cut out a paper "map" of your missionary family's country (just a rough outline will be fine). Announce that you're going to "adopt" that family. You can even make up an official-looking Certificate of Adoption. Ask the kids to write on the map everything they know about the missionary family—names, birthdays, forms of ministry, etc.

Next, look up the missionary family's country in an encyclopedia and add important data to your map. Then distribute stationery so everyone can write short letters to the missionary family, encouraging them (smaller children can dictate their messages to parents or older children). Close with prayer for your adopted family.

FRIDAY—Another Simple Activity

Create a "care package" by making or buying small gifts for each member of the missionary family and sending it to them. (Include books, squirt-guns, seeds, toothpaste, whatever kids suggest!) Let kids see Dad writing a generous check to put in the package.

SATURDAY—A Special Event

Put together a picnic lunch and go someplace for a relaxing afternoon. Be sure to give your children a chance to be helpful in preparing for the picnic. Make a point to give plenty of eye contact to your children as they talk with you. Fill their emotional tanks with good feelings of being loved by Mom and Dad.

RESOURCE SUGGESTION: For a wonderful resource book on missions, pick up a copy of *Operation World* at any Christian bookstore.

WEEK 28

Living Value for the Week: RESPONSIBILITY (To be a good citizen)
Special Celebration Day (optional): Independence Day
Scripture: Romans 13:1-7
Memory Verse: *""Well done, good and faithful servant! You have been faithful with a few things; I will put you in charge of many things."—Matthew 25:2a*

Materials: red, white, and blue crayons
                two flat lids
                chalk
                an American songbook
                pictures of famous Americans (could
                be in a book)

Ask not what your country can do for you: Ask what you can do for your country.— John Fitzgerald Kennedy

SUNDAY—A Topic Introduction
With red, white, and blue crayons, have your child draw an American flag. Display the flag proudly in a window.

MONDAY—A Simple Activity
Number nine squares with chalk on your driveway in a tic-tac-toe formation. Mark two flat lids with a plus (+) and a minus (-) and have kids stand five feet away to toss the two lids onto your grid. Total the scores in each of ten tries. High score wins. Discuss: "How would you rank our country, on a scale of 1 to 9? What do you like about our country? What do you wish could be different about our country? How do you think God feels about our country?"

86

TUESDAY—A Story Time

Read Romans 13:1-7 to your kids. Ask them to imagine with you what a "good" ruler would be like and what a "bad" ruler would be like. Then spend some time in prayer for all those who work in government.

WEDNESDAY—A Self-esteem Builder

Talk with your child about great things that famous Americans have done (Lincoln, Jefferson, Carver, King, Twain, Jonas Salk, Henry Ford, Robert Frost, or any of your favorite heroes). Ask: "If you could so something great, what would it be?" Have kids draw a picture of themselves doing something great.

THURSDAY—A Family Worship Time

Spend some time preparing a short (ten minute) history of the founding of our country. For example, my outline looked like this: 1) Pilgrims; 2) Colonies; 3) Freedom; 4) King George; 5) Representation; 6) Boston Tea Party; 7) Paul Revere's Ride; 8) Declaration of Independence; 9) Bunker Hill; 10) Revolutionary War. Talk through the reasons for Independence Day with your kids, using pictures and drawings when appropriate. Then sing some patriotic songs and close by giving thanks for our country.

FRIDAY—Another Simple Activity

Take some time to cool off and go swimming. On the way home, discuss what would be the responsiblities of a lifeguard.

SATURDAY—A Special Event

Have the kids put on their pajama's, bundle everyone in the car, and go watch some fireworks.

RESOURCE SUGGESTION: Pick up *The Timetables of American History* (Simon and Schuster) at the library. A splendid overview!

WEEK 29

Living Value for the Week: RESPECTFULNESS (Through good listening)
Character: Samuel
Scripture: 1 Samuel 3
Memory Verse: *"Speak, Lord, for your servant is listening."—*
I Samuel 3:9b

Materials:
cotton balls
paper and pencils
toothpicks
balloons
string
Tupperware lid
yardstick

The world is filled with willing people; some willing to work, the rest willing to let them.— Robert Frost

SUNDAY—A Topic Introduction

Mom starts to say, "We show respect by listening," but Dad pretends he can't hear her. After a few seconds he pulls two cotton balls from his ears. "How does good listening show that we're working together?"

MONDAY—A Simple Activity

A game that requires careful listening is "It's You!" Stand in a circle, throw a ball high into the air, and yell a name. The person named must try to catch the ball. (Make it easy for little ones to catch.)

TUESDAY—A Story Time

Tell about the events found in I Samuel 3. Samuel listens and obeys both Eli and God. Discuss: "Have you ever wished God would speak with a louder voice, like He did with Samuel? What do you think God would be saying to *you* today?"

WEDNESDAY—A Self-esteem Builder

Have everyone write two or three compliments about another family member, but keep the written words a secret. Now Dad reads one. First, try to guess who the compliment is about, then try to guess who wrote it. (You can create many variations of this game. Parents can help record little ones' comments.)

THURSDAY—A Family Worship Time

Begin by asking the children to retell the story of Samuel's listening and obeying. Then ask: "Do you ever find it hard to listen? When?" Talk with your children about specific situations in which they find it hard to listen. Create a chart with columns reading:

Situation   *If I Don't Listen*   *If I Do Listen*

Jot down a situation and imagine together what could happen in each situation if family members do, and do not, listen. This should be fun, not a time to criticize. Next, discuss: "What can I do to become a better listener?" Introduce your new memory verse and close in prayer.

FRIDAY—Another Simple Activity

Play "What Was That?" Everyone stands in a line (the more the merrier). The person on the end whispers a two-line poem to his or her neighbor, and each passes it down the line. See how it changes as it moves!

SATURDAY— A Special Event

Hold a Mini-Olympics. Events could include: toothpick javelin, balloon shot-put, lid discus, water-balloon hammer throw, standing long jump, races, and any other serious or silly events you can think up. Create fun games that your little ones can win. Give gold and silver "Hershey's Kiss" awards.

RESOURCE SUGGESTION: Dorothy Martin's *Creative Family Worship* (Moody) offers a good general introduction to family devotions.

WEEK 30

Living Value for the Week: RESPECTFULNESS (By honoring parents and others)
Character: Samuel
Scripture: I Samuel 3
Memory Verse: *"Listen, my sons, to a father's instruction; pay attention and gain understanding."—Proverbs 4:1*

Materials: crayons
paper
magazines
scissors
glue and tape
water toys

The most important thing a father can do for his children is to love their mother.— Theodore M. Hesburgh

SUNDAY—A Topic Introduction

Define the word "respect" by doing an acrostic of the word. Ask your children to help you fill in the words that begin with: R-E-S-P-E-C-T.

MONDAY—A Simple Activity

In a park or big back yard, line everyone up and give each kid a big old shoe. Have them, in turn, put on the shoe and, simply by swinging their legs, see who can kick the shoe the farthest. Discuss: "Have you ever wanted to 'kick against' Mom and Dad's rules? How do you feel at those times? What can we do to make things better for you in our family?"

TUESDAY—A Story Time

Using a Bible story book, take another look at Samuel as a boy and compare him to Eli's two sons in I Samuel 2, 3, and 4. Ask: "What makes some children turn out 'good' and some turn out 'bad'? What is it about the parents? What is it about the children themselves?"

WEDNESDAY—A Self-esteem Builder

Draw names, and then say: "Some time during the day you must honor the person whose name you chose." Make suggestions about how kids could honor another person. They could write an encouraging note, give a compliment, make a gift, help with a chore, listen to feelings. Other ideas?

THURSDAY—A Family Worship Time

Give everyone an old magazine or a simple scrapbook (with pages held together by yarn). Invite everyone to get involved creating an "honor scrapbook" for the person whose name they drew yesterday.

An honor scrapbook has pictures and drawings pasted in it, along with sayings written about the person. For example, my daughter Kaitlin's has pictures of kittens and books, a drawing of her helping Mom set the table, and honoring statements such as: "Kaitlin is a big girl" and "Kaitlin loves Jesus." Spend plenty of time creating your honor scrapbooks (perhaps over a period of days or weeks), then share them with each other.

FRIDAY—Another Simple Activity

Use your dinner table as a place for "show and tell." What one thing would you like to bring to the table and tell us about? Mom and Dad should participate, too.

SATURDAY— A Special Event

Have an afternoon of water fun. Run through a sprinkler, toss some water balloons, jump on a slip-n-slide, shoot a squirt gun . . . anything cool and fun.

RESOURCE SUGGESTION: For an inspiring, well-written autobiography, read John Owen's *This Stubborn Soil*. An excellent book!

WEEK 31

Living Value for the Week: CONCERN (Through taking care of those in need)
Character: Jesus, the Good Shepherd
Scripture: John 10:11-16
Memory Verse: *"I am the good shepherd. The good shepherd lays down his life for the sheep."—John 10:11*

Materials: paper and pens
             Burger King crown (free at any Burger King)
             index cards
             tape

Give me the ready hand rather than the ready tongue.— Giuseppe Garibaldi

SUNDAY—A Topic Introduction

Mention that one way we honor others is by showing concern and taking care of them when they need our help. Ask: "Who takes care of you when you are sick? Would you take care of me if I were sick?"

MONDAY—A Simple Activity

Do a "family problem search." Have everyone sit in a circle and simply ask: "What problems are people in our family having right now—at home, school, work?" Parents share, too. Express concern for one another by brainstorming possible solutions, and then praying about the situations.

TUESDAY—A Story Time

Ask kids to tell stories—about anything, serious or silly. Then you tell a story about a time when you felt the most concern from your parents or the most "taken care of"·by your parents (when you were a child).

Put a Burger King crown on each kid's head, in turn, and bow before them. Show concern for them by asking: "What is the one

92

thing you would like me to do for you?" (Do it, if it is within reason! Many requests will no doubt have to be modified a bit.)

WEDNESDAY—A Self-esteem Builder

Create a "World's Greatest" certificate for each child. It could be "World's Greatest Son," or "World's Greatest Helper," or any quality you want to encourage. Explain why you are giving the certificate, include an appropriate Scripture verse, and sign it. The kids might want to fill out a "World's Greatest Mom/Dad" certificate for you!

THURSDAY—A Family Worship Time

With the family gathered, read John 10:11-16 aloud. Ask everyone to spend a few moments in silence imagining: "You are a little lost sheep. You don't know how to get home. It's getting dark. It's getting cold. You're very afraid. . . . Suddenly, a strong hand picks you up and holds you close. It's the shepherd! He looks at you and says . . .".

Ask everyone to complete the sentence after two minutes of silence. Close by going to each other and saying: "Jesus, the Good Shepherd, takes care of you. He loves you very much. And so do I.."

FRIDAY—Another Simple Activity

At breakfast, draw one family member's name from a hat. This person will have the privilege of being "taken care of" by everyone else that evening. This person may decide on the evening's meal and activities. Other family members will try to be open to the cared-for person's desires and needs. Keep a good sense of humor, and approach this in the spirit of fun.

SATURDAY— A Special Event

In advance, arrange for a visit to a nursing home by calling ahead and getting suggestions about how a family could help during visitation hours. Discuss ideas with your family for things you could do to help someone who may be lonely or discouraged. Decide as a family what to do, then take the time to do it.

WEEK 32

Living Value for the Week: ENTHUSIASM (About a family vacation)
Scripture: Philippians 4:8
Memory Verse: *"Never be lacking in zeal, but keep your spiritual fervor, serving the Lord."—Romans 12:11*

Materials: grocery bags

Keep your face to the sunshine and you cannot see the shadow.— Helen Keller

SUNDAY—A Topic Introduction
Are you going on a vacation this year? Discuss where you're going and what you'll be doing on your vacation. Ask: "What attitude do we want to have while we're vacationing? What will we do if someone is grumpy?"

MONDAY—A Simple Activity
Before you leave, have each child make a "vacation bag." Using a plastic grocery bag, they stuff the special things they want to take with them into it. Put their names on their bags.

TUESDAY—A Story Time
Take along a Bible story book (preferably one with pictures) for your child to look at in the car. Ask him or her to search: "What stories talk about people traveling?" (Abraham, Joseph, Mary, Paul, etc.).

WEDNESDAY—A Self-esteem Builder
In the car, ask your children to make up a poem about Dad and recite it. (Soon everybody will be making up poems.) Then think of a simple tune ("Row, Row, Row" or "Mary Had a Little Lamb") and write new words to it that tell how someone in

your family is special. For example, "Molly is a pretty girl, pretty girl, pretty girl . . .".

THURSDAY—A Family Worship Time

While driving in the car, have someone read Philippians 4:8. "What are some of the good and excellent things we have talked about this year in our family?" Discuss as a family the favorite events, activities, games that you've enjoyed in your family devotions. Of course, this is a good time to come up with new ideas, to check memory verses, to retell Bible stories, to say things you appreciate about one another, and to sing songs.

Because vacations are a break from routine, it is easy to get grouchy, so try to be as upbeat as possible with your children. And remember: Vacations are spoiled by trying to do too much.

FRIDAY—Another Simple Activity

Play "A to Z" in your car: "I'm looking for the letter 'A' on a sign or billboard. There! Now, Colin, can you find a letter 'B'?"

SATURDAY— A Special Event

Many vacations are "hurry-hurry" times, so plan one day in which you do plan to do nothing but walk in the woods, go for a swim, or play outside together as a family. No TV, no amusement parks, no lines, and no rushing from place to place.

RESOURCE SUGGESTION: Nearly everybody likes Maranatha Music's *Psalty* and *Kid's Praise* tapes. Take some with you in the car.

WEEK 33

Living Value for the Week: FAITHFULNESS (Loving God even when afraid)
Character: David
Scripture: I Samuel 17
Memory verse: *"Even though I walk through the valley of the shadow of death, I will fear no evil, for you are with me."—Psalm 23:4a*

Materials: large sheets of butcher paper
                 crayons
                 tape
                 squirt guns
                 Nerf balls
                 party favors
                 cake and ice cream

It is better to be faithful than famous.— Theodore Roosevelt

SUNDAY—A Topic Introduction
Talk with your child about a time when you were confronted by a "bully." Tell how you felt. What did you do?

MONDAY—A Simple Activity
Go for a walk (to a place with rocks, if possible). Have everyone pick out five smooth stones and throw them at a target.

TUESDAY—A Story Time
Tell the story of David and Goliath. Make it as dramatic as you can by using your hands and body. Have very small children mimic your movements.

WEDNESDAY—A Self-esteem Builder

Put on a "family drama." Choose one person and explain that he or she is to leave while everyone else creates a mini-play about him or her. Choose one important event in that person's life and dramatize it. Then perform it for the honored guest. (This idea and the following were adapted from Wayne Rickerson.)

THURSDAY—A Family Worship Time

If you have a kid's tape with a song about David and Goliath, begin your time together by singing along with that song. There are several from which to choose.

Ask your kids to re-tell the story of David and Goliath, and act it out with them once again. Then draw a huge Goliath on a large piece of butcher paper, and as the kids color in his face, shield, and armor, discuss how God was with David, even when he was surely afraid. Ask: "Is God with us when we're afraid?"

Have everyone write one fear on Goliath, then step back and throw "stones" (Nerf balls) at him, or shoot him with squirt guns, and, finally, attack him and tear him up. Pray that we'll feel God's presence with us and stay faithful to Him, even when we are afraid.

FRIDAY—Another Simple Activity

Go to a big park and try to throw some things around with accuracy. Try using a slingshot, a frisbee, a football, and a boomerang. Talk about young David's ability to stand up to a scary giant. Ask older children: "What's the most scary 'giant' you are facing in your life right now?"

SATURDAY—A Special Event

Throw a "no reason" party. Invite some friends over and have cake and ice cream, wear party hats, blow party horns, and play a couple of simple party games like pin-the-tail and guess-the-animal.

RESOURCE SUGGESTION: Our kids have enjoyed *The Illustrated Bible Stories for Children* (Joshua Morris). Good pictures, modern language.

WEEK 34

Living Value for the Week: REVERENCE (For God's greatness)
Character: God, the Almighty
Scripture: Psalm 34:3
Memory Verse: *"Glorify the Lord with me; let us exalt his name together."—Psalm 34:*

Materials: pencils and paper
                     crayons or markers

I seem to have been only like a boy playing on the seashore and diverting myself in now and then finding the smoother pebble or a prettier shell than ordinary, whilst the great ocean of truth lay all undiscovered before me.—Isaac Newton

SUNDAY—A Topic Introduction
Ask older kids: "Of all the great things God has done, which would you say are the most 'awesome'?"

MONDAY—A Simple Activity
Go for a "great and small" walk. As you wander outside, say "Great!" when you spot a great thing, and "Small!" when you spot a small thing.

TUESDAY—A Story Time
Read Psalm 34 to your children. Then ask the older children to pretend to be God and respond to: "Tell us, God, what's it like to rule the universe? What's the most challenging?"

98

WEDNESDAY—A Self-esteem Builder

At the dinner table, go around and have everyone tell about: "The Greatest Moment of My Life." Mom and Dad could also talk about some of the *worst* moments in their lives, to add a bit of poignancy and/or humor to the discussion.

THURSDAY—A Family Worship Time

Have your oldest child read Psalm 34 to everyone. Point out that David knew the Lord was with him and could do great things, even when David was afraid. Give kids a piece of paper and crayons, asking them to draw a picture of something that shows how great God is.

After all have explained their pictures, spend a moment offering sentence praise prayers to God. Invite everyone to put their bodies in positions that show reverence for God's greatness, for example: raising hands, bowing from the waist, kneeling, laying prone on the floor (all of these are prayer positions, or attitudes of respect found in the Bible).

FRIDAY—Another Simple Activity

Ask: "What is the greatest thing you can imagine?" Parents, make a few guesses about what your child's response will be before he or she reveals it to you. Discuss: "How do we know that God is the greatest being in the universe?"

SATURDAY—A Special Event

Make a mural about the greatness of God. Use finger paints, watercolors, or markers. Get messy! While you are working on the mural, play music that suggests the greatness of creation (Holst's "The Planets" is a good choice.)

RESOURCE SUGGESTION: Use two titles in the *Ten Commandments Mysteries* (Chariot) to teach kids the value of reverence: *The Mystery of the Vanishing Present* and *The Mystery of the Second Map*.

WEEK 35

Living Value for the Week: PRAISE (For God's creative power)
Character: God, the Creator
Scripture: Psalm 8
Memory Verse: *"In the beginning God created the heavens and the earth."*—Genesis 1:1

Materials:
- nature materials
- ears of corn
- construction paper
- paper and pencils
- music tapes
- nature pictures
- a piece of clean cardboard, cut into a circle (about twelve inches in diameter)
- index cards
- a glass jar

He who praises everybody, praises nobody.— Samuel Johnson

SUNDAY—A Topic Introduction
Read Psalm 8 to your children, using music and nature pictures to create a mood of praise to God.

MONDAY—A Simple Activity
Go for a walk in a forest or a park. Ask little ones: "Who created this?" Ask older ones: "Why do you think God made these the way He did?" Collect flowers, leaves, pine cones and anything of interest to the children.

TUESDAY—A Story Time
Mom and Dad, tell your children your testimony. How did you come to love Jesus? (Try to use words that children can easily understand.)

WEDNESDAY—A Self-esteem Builder

Parents, spend a few moments writing down things you appreciate about your child. Glue these statements to a nice piece of paper that says "I appreciate you!" at the top. Give this small gift to your child, telling her that you are very glad God created her and gave her to you.

THURSDAY—A Family Worship Time

Put on some relaxing music that suggests the beautiful world our God created (Vivaldi's "Four Seasons" is nice). Now, take your cones, leaves, and flowers and create a "nature picture" by gluing them together onto your cardboard circle to make a table centerpiece. "Hasn't God created a beautiful world?"

Praise God for His creation by doing a responsive reading (parents read a line, then children read the next, in alternating fashion). You'll find many good verses in the Psalms to help you put together the reading (photocopy it in advance). Close by singing a verse of "How Great Thou Art," "Morning Has Broken," or any hymn that praises the greatness of God's creative power.

FRIDAY—Another Simple Activity

A fun game to try: Buy a couple ears of corn and have your kids try to shuck them using only their feet. Talk about the miracle of food. God has created so many good things for us to eat.

SATURDAY—A Special Event

With school about to start, get the kids thinking about their plans and desires for the next twelve months. Give everyone three index cards and ask them to write their ideas for "fun things we want to try this year." Put the cards into a specially decorated "fun jar" and promise to pull one out each month to try the idea.

RESOURCE SUGGESTION: *Wonderful Earth* (Chariot) has pictures that pop out, flaps that lift, colorful illustrations. It's a great book for teaching kids the greatness of God's creation.

WEEK 36

Living Value for the Week: CONFIDENCE (As school starts)
Scripture: Mark 4:35-41
Memory Verse: *"Why are you so afraid? Do you still have no faith?"—Mark 4:40*

Materials: camera
index cards and pencils
construction paper

It is wonderful what strength of purpose and boldness and energy of will are roused by the assurance that we are doing our duty.— Walter Scott

SUNDAY—A Topic Introduction

Pray with your child, that the new school year will be a success, that they will glorify God through their friendships and their schoolwork—and that they will enjoy themselves.

MONDAY—A Simple Activity

Since many school years begin with a standard essay, take this last day together and help your child create an outline about: "What I did during the summer break." This will be fun and helpful.

TUESDAY—A Story Time

Tell the story of Jesus calming the storm. Explain the story in terms of what it has meant to you in the past to be confident of God in a fearful situation. Be specific about details in your example, and invite questions from the kids about your feelings at the time.

WEDNESDAY—A Self-esteem Builder

Put an encouraging note in your childrens' lunch boxes. Remind them that you are praying for them, or just tell them you love them and that they are special.

THURSDAY—A Family Worship Time

Make this an extra-fun night, now that your kids are back in school. Begin by asking them about school: What subjects do they like best so far? Do they have any neighborhood friends in their classes ? What scares or worries them?

Ask one of the kids to read Mark 4:35-41 aloud. Say: "Suppose you are one of the disciples, and Jesus is sleeping near you. You call out: 'Teacher, don't you care if I . . . ?" (see vs. 38). How would you complete that sentence?"

After you get kids' responses, remind them that Jesus is always with them, even at times when it may seem that He isn't paying attention.

FRIDAY—Another Simple Activity

Use construction paper to tape a set of football goal posts on a bedroom wall or on the side of the refrigerator. Show your kids the goalpost and give them some index cards. Ask them to write one school-related goal on each card and tape it up under the goalpost. When someone achieves a goal, you'll move the card over the goalpost. Give lots of encouragement when someone "scores."

SATURDAY—A Special Event

Have a "Polaroid Scavenger Hunt." Make a list of twenty crazy pictures you're to get, worth various points. Mom takes one team, Dad the other. Set a two-hour time limit. Ideas: Your picture in a shoe store; in front of a fountain; in a police car (with flashing lights on: add 100 points); sitting on top of a football helmet, etc. Get the photo's developed at a one-hour developing shop and enjoy looking at the creative shots together.

RESOURCE SUGGESTION: A couple of used hymnbooks and songbooks will help your children learn the songs of faith.

WEEK 37

Living Value for the Week: FRIENDLINESS (By being polite)
Character: Joseph
Scripture: Genesis 37
Memory Verse: *"A friend loves at all times."*—*Proverbs 17:17a*

Materials:
- Ping-Pong balls
- colorful construction paper
- a poster board
- cookie recipe and ingredients
- paper cups
- pencils
- buttons
- ball of yarn

Real friends are those who, when you make a fool of yourself, don't think you've done a permanent job.

SUNDAY—A Topic Introduction
Ask, and discuss: "What does the word 'polite' mean to you? Tell about someone you know that has been polite to you. When was the last time you were polite to a friend? How does being polite help someone make friends?"

MONDAY—A Simple Activity
Play "Family Pool." Tape a paper cup to each corner of your dining room table and a cup to each side. Assign different points to each "pocket." Using pencils as cue sticks, players try to shoot Ping-Pong balls into the pockets. Rotate players with each shot, and allow twenty tries per person for each game. Talk about how politeness relates to sports competitiveness.

TUESDAY—A Story Time
Describe the events in Genesis 37. Then invite family members to tell about times when they have been mistreated at home, school, or work. Discuss: "How are our experiences like and unlike what happened to Joseph? If you were Joseph, how would you have felt? How do you respond to those who are unfriendly with you?"

WEDNESDAY—A Self-esteem Builder

On special days we give flowers. With this idea in mind, make an "appreciation bouquet." First, decide who will receive your family's bouquet gift. Cut flower petals from colored paper, and on each petal have everyone write: "I appreciate you for _____ ." In the center circle write the name of the honored person. Use wire to make a stem.

THURSDAY—A Family Worship Time

Since the baseball play-offs are coming up, why not play "Bible Baseball" with your family tonight? Give each child a Bible and sit in a circle. Draw a baseball diamond on poster board and give each person a button "player" that moves around the bases. Dad calls out a Scripture reference, then says "Go!" The first person to find the verse and read it gets to move his or her player to the next base. Getting "home" scores one point. Play down the competition, and play up the fun and friendliness.

FRIDAY—Another Simple Activity

Sit in a circle. Holding a ball of yarn, begin a story about your family. Toss the yarn to someone else, who must continue the story. Keep this up until everyone has had a chance to talk at least once.

Later, unravel some of the yarn and have everyone hold part of it. Mention that a family can be tied together very closely, through love, and through the Spirit of Christ who lives in each family member. Pray that the bond of unity in your family will continue to get stronger.

SATURDAY—A Special Event

Have the family bake cookies together. Choose a recipe (you'll like the toll-house recipe on a Nestle's chocolate chip bag) and teach your kids how to mix the ingredients, drop the cookies, and bake. Then visit a friend's home and share the cookies.

RESOURCE SUGGESTION: Consider *Bible Stories Just My Size*, a series by Chariot, for children ages one to three. One of the books, *Joseph's Coat*, teaches the Living Value of forgiveness that comes through in Joseph's life story.

WEEK 38

Living Value for the Week: GENTLENESS
Character: Jesus
Scripture: Isaiah 53
Memory Verse: *"Take my yoke upon you and learn from me, for I am gentle and humble in heart, and you will find rest for your souls."—Matthew 11:29*

Materials: paper and pencil
index cards
newspaper ads
magazines

This is the final test of a gentleman: his respect for those who can be of no possible service to him.— William Lyon Phelps

SUNDAY—A Topic Introduction
At the table, make a list of table manners with your children. Ask: "What would a dinner party be like if there were no such thing as manners?" Inject some humor by having children role play some examples.

MONDAY—A Simple Activity
Have a contest to see who can build the highest "house of cards" with index cards. Mom and Dad try, too. Talk about this activity as a "gentleness-builder": we can't rush or be rough when trying to balance cards on top of each other. Ask: "Why does it feel good to be around someone who is gentle?"

TUESDAY—A Story Time
Tonight, before bedtime, gather with children and tell them a

story from your childhood about a time when you fought back, or *didn't* fight back. Talk about how you felt. Ask: "How is being gentle different from being afraid?"

WEDNESDAY—A Self-esteem Builder

Gather together and ask everyone: "If you could be any flower in the world, what would you be? Why? Where would you be? Who would pick you?"

THURSDAY—A Family Worship Time

Read Isaiah 53 to your gathered family. Tell kids that you are going to read through the passage again. This time, whenever they hear a phrase that tells them that the Servant (Jesus) was gentle—did not fight back—they should raise their hands. Stop and acknowledge each child's raised hand and comments before continuing to read.

Take a moment to explain the importance of Christ's gentleness to the plan of salvation: He willingly gave up His power in order to die for us.

FRIDAY—Another Simple Activity

Show your children a silent film (or a cartoon with the sound off). Then give them a cassette recorder and ask them to create a sound tract for the video—dialogue, sound effects, etc. Great fun!

SATURDAY—A Special Event

Invite friends over for dessert and games (and a chance for your family to practice your manners and gentleness with others). Make sure to "debrief" your children later; talking with them about what they did, how others responded, and how they felt about it.

ACTIVITY SUGGESTION: Invite young children to pray often. Toddlers love to pray long prayers—"Thank You for the dog, the walls, the grass, the table, the spoons . . ."—but school-agers are more comfortable with sentence prayers.

WEEK 39

Living Value for the Week: HUMILITY (By considering others' feelings)
Character: Jesus
Scripture: Philippians 2:4-11
Memory Verse: *"Do nothing out of selfish ambition or vain conceit, but in humility consider others better than yourselves."*—*Philippians 2:3*

Materials: balloon
a fan
newspapers or magazines
tape
scissors
paper
crayons

It was pride that changed angels into devils; it is humility that makes men as angels.—Augustine

SUNDAY—A Topic Introduction

Ask, and discuss: "How do you like to be treated? What do I do that makes you feel special? What do I do that makes you feel afraid or ashamed?" Be ready to take seriously the kids' answers to all three questions. This can be an exercise in humility for parents.

MONDAY—A Simple Activity

Give your child a balloon and a fan (a record album cover works well). He or she must fan the balloon, without touching it, around a pre-selected course without the balloon touching the floor. With older children, talk about what it means to "keep up" appearances around others.

TUESDAY—A Story Time

Ask the little ones to tell about a time when they shared toys with someone else. Was that hard to do? Why?

WEDNESDAY—A Self-esteem Builder

Ask your child to use pictures cut from magazines or newspapers in order to create a collage entitled, "Today I Am Feeling . . .". Talk about the feelings that come through. Just listen, and respond with hugs and holding as appropriate.

THURSDAY—A Family Worship Time

Read aloud Philippians 2:4-11. Explain what the passage says about Jesus' humility and what the passage means for us today.

Then ask for specific examples of conflicts family members are facing. After each situation is fully described, consider together: "What would Jesus do?" Bring out the true nature of the humility exemplified by Jesus.

FRIDAY—Another Simple Activity

Ask your kids to decide, along with their friends, on a special thing to do today—perhaps go somewhere in Mom's care for fun. But let your kids know that this will be an opportunity to practice "considering others' ideas as important as our own." Can they exercise humility in agreeing with other's desires?

SATURDAY—A Special Event

Have a "pajama party." After everyone is ready for bed, make some popcorn and punch. Lay close to your child for awhile and talk about how Jesus gave up His home in heaven to be close to us.

RESOURCE SUGGESTION: Cheryl Biehl's *Scriptural Meditation* (Questar) will deepen your spiritual life. It's a truly profound book.

WEEK 40

Living Value for the Week: THANKFULNESS
Characters: Ten Lepers
Scripture: Luke 17:11-19
Memory Verse: *"Give thanks in all circumstances, for this is God's will for you in Christ Jesus."—I Thessalonians 5:18*

Materials:
- gold spray paint
- colored pencils
- poison ivy (or a picture of poison ivy)
- Play-Doh
- paper

I have concluded that the accumulation of wealth is an insufficient reason for living. . . . I will consider my earthly existence to have been wasted unless I can recall a loving family, a consistent investment in the lives of people, and an earnest attempt to serve the God who made me.—Dr. James Dobson

SUNDAY—A Topic Introduction

Teach your child a simple poem:

> All things bright and beautiful,
>> All creatures great and small,
> All things wise and wonderful,
>> The Lord God made them all.

Ask: "Of all the things God has made, name five of them that you are most thankful for."

MONDAY—A Simple Activity

Give your children Play-Doh and ask them to make a person. When they are done, praise their work and ask, "It is hard, isn't it? Can you make a real person? Imagine how hard it must be to make a real person! Who can do it? God can! Are you glad He made you?"

TUESDAY—A Story Time

Tell a story from your personal experience about a time when you received a thank-you note. Include: What gift had you given? Why did this note mean so much to you? How do you feel when a gift seems to generate no thankfulness in return?

WEDNESDAY—A Self-esteem Builder

Gather the smaller children and tie a ribbon around the waste of each one. Make a pretty bow, so they end up being gift-wrapped. Ask: "Why do you think I made you look like a present?" After getting their responses, tell them that you consider children to be a gift from the Lord. Tell them you are so thankful to God for each one of them. Give out lots of hugs.

THURSDAY—A Family Worship Time

Show kids some poison ivy (or a picture of it) and give some facts about it. If you've ever been infected with a poison ivy rash, describe your experience in detail. Ouch! Then ask kids to share stories about times they've had chicken pox, or rashes, itches, etc.

Read the story of the ten lepers, from Luke 17:11-19. Ask: "What would it be like if you had 'poison ivy skin' but you could be 'healed' with just a touch from a stranger? How thankful would you be? Would you say thank-you?" (Note: Older kids may want to know facts about leprosy, so be prepared for that.)

FRIDAY—Another Simple Activity

Find a spider web and spray it with gold spray-paint. Then lift a piece of construction paper onto it, causing it to stick and creating a nice nature picture.

SATURDAY—A Special Event

Collect some fallen leaves, place them under white paper, and rub with colored pencils to make leaf rubbings. Take your beautiful harvest pictures to grandparents or special friends.

RESOURCE SUGGESTION: Joyce Becker's *Bible Crafts* (Holiday House) offers a variety of ideas for making the Bible come to life for children.

111

WEEK 41

Living Value for the Week: KINDNESS (Toward someone who feels alone)
Character: Ruth
Scripture: Ruth 1:1-22
Memory Verse: *"Be kind and compassionate to one another, forgiving each other, just as in Christ God forgave you."—Ephesians 4:32*

Materials:　　　finger paints
　　　　　　　　paper
　　　　　　　　index cards
　　　　　　　　pencils

SUNDAY—A Topic Introduction

Don't wait until the funeral to send flowers.—Scottish proverb

Some time during the day ask each of your children to play alone, apart from anyone else, for a while. Tell them you want to talk later about how it feels to be alone. Later, ask questions like: "How did it feel to be alone? When have you felt the most alone? Have you ever had someone stay with you when you were alone—just to make you feel better?"

MONDAY—A Simple Activity

Ask your kids to look out the window, then finger paint a picture of what they see. If your kids are older, have them use watercolors. Talk about how God has made everything dependent on other things. Can they tell how? (Examples: trees need the sun; birds need the trees; clouds need water, etc.) Point out that people need other people. That's why we work on being kind.

TUESDAY—A Story Time

Mom and Dad, in turn, tell about a time when you felt the most alone. What did you wish would happen? Was anyone kind enough to help you, stay with you? If not, how did you get through this time?

WEDNESDAY—A Self-esteem Builder

Ask your kids to paint or draw a self-portrait. (Self-portraits can reveal quite a bit about how a children feel about himself themselves.) After they've completed their pictures, talk with them about what the portraits reveal. Say: "Now draw in someone who you like to be close to when you are feeling lonely."

THURSDAY—A Family Worship Time

Read Ruth 1:1-22. See who can tell the most ways that Ruth was being kind to Naomi.

Then suddenly announce: "You've just become a member of the 'Kindness Konspiracy.' Your job is to secretly do something kind for someone else in the family. It must be secret—nobody is to know you did it." Talk about being kind to others because Christ has been kind to us, then share family ideas for being kind during the Kindness Konspiracy. Give everyone twenty-four hours to do something kind for someone else. Close with prayer.

FRIDAY—Another Simple Activity

Ask kids to report: "Did you do something kind for someone in the family during the last twenty-four hours? Don't tell us what you did, but do tell us how it made you feel. If no one will ever know you did that kind thing, how does that make you feel?"

SATURDAY—A Special Event

Give each of your children a "grown-up" chore to do with either Mom or Dad. Make sure it is something a bit out of the ordinary (like building something or cleaning the garage). Talk with kids about their kindness as you work.

RESOURCE SUGGESTION: For great family reading, try *Anne of Green Gables* by Lucy Maud Montgomery.

WEEK 42

Living Value for the Week: KINDNESS
Character: Ruth
Scripture: Ruth 2
Memory Verse: *"Be kind and compassionate to one another, forgiving each other, just as in Christ God forgave you."—Ephesians 4:32*

Materials: paper and marking pens
kids' Christian music tapes
a glass jar
index cards
pencils

Kindness is a language the dumb can speak and the deaf can hear and understand.—Christian Nestell Bovee

SUNDAY—A Topic Introduction
Surprise children by giving them something they would normally have to ask for first: "Would anybody like an ice cream cone?"

MONDAY—A Simple Activity
With your children's help, write down on index cards some simple ideas for being kind to others this fall. Put the ideas into a jar, mix them up, and pull one out. Put the idea into practice as soon as possible. Let your kids know that they can be kind servants for God.

TUESDAY—A Story Time
Read Ruth 2:1-23 to your family. Then sit in a circle and retell the action in Ruth 2 as a revolving story. Dad begins, gets the characters to a climactic point, and then the person on his left

114

picks it up. Go around the circle, each adding to the story, until all have had a turn. (Parents can "prime the pump" as needed, with an occasional "Then what happened?")

WEDNESDAY—A Self-esteem Builder

Help your children create a personal "coat of arms" for themselves. Put their names on the top, and have them fill four squares of a shield with pictures of: 1) their best day ever, 2) their favorite fun activity, 3) their biggest dream, and 4) themselves doing something kind. On the drape at the bottom they should write their own personal "motto."

THURSDAY—A Family Worship Time

Tonight teach your kids to use Bible tools. First, show them a concordance and explain how it works (all references to the word "kind" are grouped together; a partial sentence is shown using a "k" to represent "kind"). Read a few of the sentences and see who can look them up in a Bible. Next, show kids a Bible dictionary and suggest they look up a few references (try Ruth, Moab, and threshing). Then get out a Bible atlas and help them find Judah and Jerusalem. Finally, show the kids additional information found in a study Bible (outlines, dates, author information, etc.).

FRIDAY—Another Simple Activity

Give your kids an assignment that usues what they learned yesterday: After a half hour with the Bible reference tools, what can they tell you about the Book of Ruth?

SATURDAY—A Special Event

Watching a play is a wonderful way to develop young minds. Have your kids read a play, then take them to see it.

RESOURCE SUGGESTION: For a wonderful book that teaches the value of kindness, try *Suzy Swoof* (Chariot) with your young children, age three to eight.

WEEK 43

Living Value for the Week: UNSELFISHNESS
Character: A poor widow
Scripture: Mark 12:41-44
Memory Verse: *"For I have come down from heaven not to do my will but to do the will of him who sent me."—John 6:38*

Materials: a big canvas or plastic bag
               old newspapers
               Popsicle sticks
               marking pens
               a copy of your church's financial report
               family scrapbook
               family prayer notebook

The one who lives by himself and for himself is likely to be corrupted by the company he keeps.— Charles H. Parkhurst

SUNDAY—A Topic Introduction
Tell the children: "One of the most unselfish things we can do for people is to use some of our time to pray for them. Who do we know that needs our prayers?"

MONDAY—A Simple Activity
Fill a big bag with wadded newspapers, so it looks huge and heavy. Call your younger children into the room and say, "Oh! I've got this heavy burden. Who will help me get rid of it?" Tell them one of your burdens that they can pray for. Then give the burden to your child and ask, "What burden do you have that I can pray for?"

TUESDAY—A Story Time
Tell a story about a time when you had to give up something

116

that was very valuable to you. Did you do it willingly? Why, or why not? How hard was it to give away something you wanted to keep?

WEDNESDAY—A Self-esteem Builder

Just before bedtime, offer to give kids massages. Make bedtime appointments with each child to rub out aches and pains in feet, legs, arms, and backs. Don't forget to end with a gentle scalp massage. See how your children relax and glow after warm, loving touches from Mom or Dad! Most kidswill fall asleep immediately.

THURSDAY—A Family Worship Time

Read the story of "The Widow's Offering," from Mark 12:41-43. Spend a few moments talking about the importance of giving. Since children can be confused about what happens to the money in offering plates on Sunday morning, let them study a church budget report that shows where your offering money goes.

Later, show your kids a record of your own family's giving to church and/or other worthy causes. Invite any questions they may have about family finances and how spending decisions are made in your family.

FRIDAY—Another Simple Activity

Give each of your kids an amount of money in an envelope marked: My Helping Hand. Tell the kids to keep the money for as long as they want, until they have an opportunity to spend it on someone else.

SATURDAY—A Special Event

Spend an hour updating your family prayer book and your family scrapbook. Then rent a good children's movie and enjoy an evening of viewing and discussing together (suggestions: "Anne of Green Gables," "Swiss Family Robinson," "Chariots of Fire").

ACTIVITY SUGGESTION: Have you ever taken your children to a concert? Many theaters offer special family matinee's for less money.

WEEK 44

Living Values for the Week: CONVICTION (That God keeps His promises)
Special Celebration Days (optional): All Saint's Day / Halloween
Characters: Many biblical heroes
Scripture: Hebrews 11
Memory Verse: *"O Sovereign Lord, you are God! Your words are trustworthy, and you have promised these good things to your servant."—II Samuel 7:28*

Materials: pen and paper
                     Jello
                     pots and pans, spoons
                     cookie cutters
                     pumpkins
                     knife
                     apples and caramel
                     large pan of water
                     string

All Saint's Day is a celebration of the faith and dedication in the lives of godly men and women. Let's return to that focus during the Halloween season.

SUNDAY—A Topic Introduction
Ask, and discuss: "Who do you want to be like when you grow up? Why?"

MONDAY—A Simple Activity
Give your older children an assignment for this week: They are to interview one adult that they trust (not their parents) and ask about this person's life and his or her convictions about God and His promises. Invite this person to your home for the interview.

TUESDAY—A Story Time

Read Hebrews 11 to your family. Tell kids that every time a "Hero of the Faith" is mentioned by name, the reading must stop while everyone cheers loudly. Be creative in your cheering—use pots, pans, and spoons to make a big, joyful racket.

WEDNESDAY—A Self-esteem Builder

Ask your child to write ten words that best describes herself, then ten more words that best describe your family, and finally five words that she hopes will describe her when she grows up.

THURSDAY—A Family Worship Time

Write your memory verse on a chalkboard or poster board and have everyone say it together. Then erase a few words and see if everyone can say it. Continue until the chalkboard is erased and everyone can say the verse.

FRIDAY—Another Simple Activity

Remind everyone of the heroes in Hebrews 11. "What made all of those people special?" (the conviction that God keeps His promises). "Do we have faith in God?" Finally, mix together packets of Jello to make finger-jello and mold them into shapes or cut them with cookie cutters. While doing this, ask, "Does God want to mold us? How does He do it?" Close by praying together.

SATURDAY—A Special Event

Throw an alternative Halloween party! Rather than going trick-or-treating, stay home and invite friends to join you to bob-for-apples, eat apples-on-a-string, make caramel apples, carve happy-faced pumpkins, and play games.

RESOURCE SUGGESTION: Get your kids interested in all the heroes of the faith. Try out *My Bible Alphabet Book* (Chariot). This rhyming book highlights the great men and women of the Bible from A to Z. For children ages two to four.

WEEK 45

Living Value for the Week: TRUST
Character: David
Scripture: Psalms 24 and 25
Memory Verse: *"To you, O Lord, I lift up my soul; in you I trust, O my God."—Psalm 25:1*

Materials: paper and pencils
                    ink pad, stampers
                    calendar
                    nickels or pennies

I always prefer to believe the best of everybody—it saves so much trouble.— Rudyard Kipling

SUNDAY—A Topic Introduction

Ask: "Do you know why I trust God? Because . . .". (Give your child a couple of your reasons, using examples of times when God has proved Himself trustworthy).

MONDAY—A Simple Activity

Provide an ink pad and some stampers, and let your kids create "stamp pictures." Discuss: "What 'marks' us as a family that trusts in God? How has God put His 'stamp' on us?"

TUESDAY—A Story Time

Invite Dad to tell a story about a time when he trusted someone and found that this person was, or was *not*, trustworthy. What happened? What did Dad learn from the experience?

WEDNESDAY—A Self-esteem Builder

Using an ink pad, have your children ink their fingers and *carefully* make copies of their fingerprints on clean paper. Examine the prints, then ask: "Did you know everyone's fingerprints

120

are different? What are yours like?" Let the kids talk about themselves; listen with lots of eye contact and gestures of approval.

Tell your kids that one thing you appreciate about them is that they can be trusted. Give a specific example of this.

THURSDAY—A Family Worship Time

Have one of your children read Psalm 24 aloud. Say: "Name three things this psalm tells us about God." Next, read Psalm 25, then sing it (it's been put to a familiar tune: "Unto thee, O Lord, Do I lift up my soul . . ."). Say: "These psalms tell us that God is great and can be trusted. What do you know about David, the man who wrote them? How did he learn to trust the Lord?"

After discussing these questions, close by asking your children what situations they face in which they need to trust God (examples: heavy schoolwork loads, bullies, worries about friends). Pray with them about these situations.

FRIDAY—Another Simple Activity

Place a calendar on the floor, stand three feet away and throw a nickel at it. Players score the number of the box they land on. Give everyone five tries. Total players' points and determine the winner. Discuss: "Does God know what's going to happen tomorrow? Next week? Next year? How does that help you trust Him?"

SATURDAY—A Special Event

Go to a shopping mall with your family. Give everyone a pencil and paper and ask them to write down ten things that people will buy that will be used up or thrown away within a few weeks. Talk with your kids about what lasts and what doesn't, about what can be trusted and what can't.

RESOURCE SUGGESTION: Parents can help their children begin a devotional life while the kids are still in their high chairs. Consider Chariot's *High Chair Devotions* series.

WEEK 46

Living Value for the Week: THANKFULNESS (Because God loves us)
Character: David
Scripture: Psalm 19
Memory Verse: *"The heavens declare the glory of God; the skies proclaim the work of his hands."—Psalm 19:1*

Materials: paper
                    safety pins
                    marking pens

Gratitude is the heart's memory.
— French Proverb

SUNDAY—A Topic Introduction

Mom and Dad each bring something to "show and tell" at the dinner table. Tell about why you are thankful for these items. Explain the place of God's love and provision in your lives, giving concrete examples.

MONDAY—A Simple Activity

Cut out small circles that are three inches in diameter. Have your kids write "God loves me!" on them and pin them to their shirts.

TUESDAY—A Story Time

Read Psalm 19 to your family. Ask, and discuss: "What would your life be like if there were no God?"

WEDNESDAY—A Self-esteem Builder

Write "God loves me," in acrostic fashion, down the left side of sheets of paper and give them to your children. Ask them to think of words and phrases that tell of all the ways God loves them. They should use these words and phrases to fill in the acrostic.

THURSDAY—A Family Worship Time

Have "home church" tonight. Talk to your children during dinner about how we should prepare for church. "What will help us get ready for church this week?" Discuss.

Later, start your home church service. You can create it however you see fit, but here is a suggested outline:

1. Opening praise: bow or kneel in silence before God for one minute
2. Welcome each other, with hugs and kisses
3. Share joys and concerns, then pray
4. Take an offering (place food items in a box for the local food
    pantry?)
5. Special music: kids sing solos or play musical selections
6. Sermon: Dad or Mom asks questions about how Psalm 19 relates to us today
9. Closing praise: one minute of applause—clap hands—for God

FRIDAY—Another Simple Activity

Ask your little ones to pretend they are animals and you'll guess what they are. You can ask school-age kids to choose a body part and talk about how wonderful it is.

SATURDAY—A Special Event

Ask kids what you could do this Saturday that would make them feel thankful at the end of the day. Go ahead and do what they suggest.

RESOURCE SUGGESTION: For teaching kids thankfulness, consider the *Kids Around the World* series, by Chariot Books. These books teach little ones about different countries, with each child thanking God for something familiar from his or her culture.

WEEK 47

Living Value for the Week: THANKFULNESS (For God's goodness and help)
Special Celebration Day (optional): Thanksgiving
Scripture: Psalm 100
Memory Verse: *"God is our refuge and strength, an ever-present help in trouble."—Psalm 46:1*

Materials:　　　colored paper
　　　　　　　　marking pens
　　　　　　　　a pack of Lifesaver candies
　　　　　　　　large sheets of brown paper
　　　　　　　　tape

If you haven't all the things you want, be grateful for all you don't have that you don't want.—Marty Radcliff

SUNDAY—A Topic Introduction

Cut colored paper into small strips. Have everyone write the things for which they are thankful on these, and make a chain from them. Hang the chain in your home as a "thankfulness reminder."

MONDAY—A Simple Activity

Hand out Lifesaver candies to everyone. Mom and Dad, and older kids, can talk about: "How Jesus is my personal Life Saver."

TUESDAY—A Story Time

Read Psalm 100 to your family, and have everyone sing "We Gather Together." Tell a story about the last time your extended family gathered together. Even if it was a sad occasion (like a funeral), talk about how God has been good to you in all circumstances.

WEDNESDAY—A Self-esteem Builder

Bless your children! Parents, call a child to you and say: "I just wanted you to feel how thankful I am for you." Sit or kneel down, and ask your child to stand before you and close his or her eyes. Place your hands gently and lovingly on the child's head for a moment; on the child's face; on the child's shoulders; on the child's arms; on the child's hands. "My blessing upon you. May God's blessing be upon you as well." Give a hug and a smile. "Go back to play!"

THURSDAY—A Family Worship Time

Put two cranberries beside each plate. As you sit around your Thanksgiving meal, pass a Bible around and have everyone read a verse from Psalm 19. Then pray that God would give all of you thankful hearts. Pass a plate around the table, asking each person to drop their cranberries onto it while stating the two things for which they are most thankful.

FRIDAY—Another Simple Activity

Draw a turkey on brown paper, make an orange feather, and play "pin the feather on the turkey." Ask: "How thankful do you think the pilgrim's were when they had their first turkey dinner in America?"

SATURDAY—A Special Event

You can teach your children to feel thankful by giving them opportunities to help others. Start saving money for a "family ministry fund" that you can give to a needy group at Thanksgiving time. Make sure your kids do things to earn money for this fund.

RESOURCE SUGGESTION: Don't miss Alice Dalgliesh's story of a pilgrim family, *The Thanksgiving Story* (Scribners).

WEEK 48

Living Value for the Week: FELLOWSHIP (With missionary workers)
Scripture: III John 5-8
Memory Verse: *"We ought therefore to show hospitality to such men so that we may work together for the truth."*—*III John 8*

Materials:

> missionary photo's and letters
> stationery
> a shoe box
> large box
> brown wrapping paper
> tape

**The best portion of a good man's life is his little, nameless, unremembered acts of kindness and of love.
—William Wordsworth**

SUNDAY—A Topic Introduction
Pass around pictures of your adopted missionary family as you read their latest letters.

MONDAY—A Simple Activity
Give stationery to your children and ask them each to write a letter to your adopted missionary family.

TUESDAY—A Story Time
Read 3 John 5-8 and explain the biblical context—the ancient story behind these verses. Check a Bible commentary to get your facts straight.

WEDNESDAY—A Self-esteem Builder
Give your child a shoe box and ask him or her to spend a few

minutes putting all of his or her favorite things (or "the things that make you most happy") into it. Ask your child to bring the box to the dinner table and tell about the things and why they are favorites. (This exercise can make for memorable meals.)

THURSDAY—A Family Worship Time

Do some investigating into what kinds of meals are served in your missionary family's country. Fix that meal (it should be simple, although possibly very spicy) and encourage your family to eat it in a way that would be customary for the particular culture involved. That is, if nationals normally eat squatting on the floor, tonight your family will eat that same way. Be aware that you will probably not be using any butter or meat, and you may be using chopsticks or simple wooden spoons—or fingers. Talk about your adopted missionary family, imagine what they are experiencing this night, and spend time praying for them.

FRIDAY—Another Simple Activity

Ask each person to make something for your adopted missionary family that encourages and indicates your fellowship and support. It might be a simple colored picture, something sewn or carved, or a poem done in calligraphy.

SATURDAY—A Special Event

Put your home-made gifts into a box, along with a few carefully selected Christmas gifts for your missionary family. Drop in your letters, wrap it up, and have everyone go with you to the post office to mail the package.

ACTIVITY SUGGESTION: Keep globes, maps, and photo's of other countries around your home, so that your child learns of our world.

WEEK 49

Living Value for the Week: JOYFULNESS
Special Celebration Days (optional): First Week of Advent
Character: Jesus
Scripture: Isaiah 9
Memory Verse: *"For to us a child is born, to us a son is given, and the government will be on his shoulders. And he will be called Wonderful Counselor, Mighty God, Everlasting Father, Prince of Peace."—Isaiah 9:6*

Materials:
    a jigsaw puzzle
    cassette tape and recorder
    wrapping paper and string
    five candles, styrofoam circle, greenery
    construction paper and marking pens

In this world, our joys are only the tender shadows which our sorrows cast. —Henry Ward Beecher

SUNDAY—A Topic Introduction
Record yourself reading Isaiah 9 on tape, and add appropriate background music to it. Play your tape for the family tonight.

MONDAY—A Simple Activity
Get out a big jigsaw puzzle and put it in a place where it can sit for a long time. Leave it out for the next few weeks, working on it alone or with friends.

TUESDAY—A Story Time
Read Isaiah 9:1-7 to your family. "This was written four hundred years before Jesus was born." Explain how the message of this passage ties the Old Testament to the New.

128

WEDNESDAY—A Self-esteem Builder

Give each person a piece of Christmas wrapping paper. Draw names. Now fold, tear, or design the paper in such a way that it will tell something about the person whose name was drawn. (For example, if I drew Molly, I'd cut mine into the shape of a kitty because Molly loves kitties.) Display and explain yur shapes.

THURSDAY—A Family Worship Time

Make an advent wreath. Push four colored candles into a one-inch-thick styrofoam base (you may need to cut triangular holes for the candles to be placed in). Place a tall white candle in the center. Decorate the base with greens that the kids bring in from outdoors. One candle will be lit each week leading up to Christmas, with the center candle lit on Christmas morning. The lighting should be accompanied by singing and Scripture readings that relate to the themes below. Traditionally, the candles are lit in this order:

Week 1: Green (representing Christ's life)—light this candle tonight

Week 2: Purple or Blue (representing Christ's royalty)

Week 3: Red (representing Christ's blood)

Week 4: Black (representing Christ's death)

Christmas Day: White (representing Christ's holiness)

FRIDAY—Another Simple Activity

Relax, and be joyful! Get kids involved in telling "silly sories." Start them off with one of your own.

SATURDAY—A Special Event

Have the kids cut out paper stars and print a memory verse (from past weeks) on each one. Punch a small hole at the top of each star and loop string through to hang on the Christmas tree. Invite kids to hang these ornaments on your tree, reciting a verse as each star is hung.

WEEK 50

Living Value for the Week: PURPOSEFULNESS (In preparation)
Special Celebration Days (optional): Second Week of Advent
Character: Jesus
Scripture: Luke 1:26-38
Memory Verse: *"But when the time had fully come, God sent his Son, born of a woman, born under law, to redeem those under law."—Galatians 4:4, 5a*

Materials:
    popcorn
    paper and marking pens
    cranberries
    String
    Christmas storybooks
    greenery

Great minds have purposes, others have wishes.—Washington Irving

SUNDAY—A Topic Introduction
Begin reading Christmas stories to your children. (Dickens' *A Christmas Carol* is good, although there are dozens of others).

MONDAY—A Simple Activity
Make creative Christmas tree ornaments: pop and string popcorn; string cranberries and hang them; make cedar or fir swags tied with red ribbon.

TUESDAY—A Story Time
Tell a story about a time when you failed to be prepared. What happened? What did you learn? Read portions of Luke 1 to your family. Focus on the various kinds of preparation that went before the birth of Christ, before the time "had fully come."

130

WEDNESDAY—A Self-esteem Builder

Take one child shopping at a time during the coming weeks—just you and he or she. Have children bring their money and help them buy gifts; take them to lunch; and take them around to see the sights and sounds of Christmas in your community. Talk about how much preparation it takes to make your family's celebration of Christmas special.

THURSDAY—A Family Worship Time

Light your advent candle for this second week of Advent, the purple or blue candle representing Christ's royalty. Then read Luke 1:26-38 aloud.

Later, begin making a creche (a nativity set) from paper, spools, wood scraps, cardboard, tubing, or whatever you have available. Make sure to include Joseph, Mary, the baby Jesus, an ox, lamb, shepherds and sheep, an angel, and three wise men. A home-made set will have much more value to your family than a store-bought plaster set.

FRIDAY—Another Simple Activity

Drive around in the car tonight and look at all of the Christmas decorations. Then come home and enjoy some hot chocolate together.

SATURDAY—A Special Event

Practice four Christmas carols (you'll find "Away In A Manger," "Silent Night," "Jingle Bells," and "We Wish You A Merry Christmas" to be easiest for the little kids). Invite another family or two to go caroling with you around your neighborhood. Bring musical instruments if you play them.

RESOURCE SUGGESTION: *Christmas Cooking Around the World*, by Susan Purdy (Watts) will give you many ideas for feasting!

WEEK 51

Living Value for the Week: PRAISE
Special Celebration Days (optional): Third Week of Advent
Character: Jesus
Scripture: Luke 2:1-20
Memory Verse: *"Glory to God in the highest, and on earth peace to men on whom his favor rests." Luke 2:14*

Materials: birthday cards
                  birthday cake
                  paper and pencils

'Twas much, that man was made like God before.But, that God should be made like man, much more.—John Donne

SUNDAY—A Topic Introduction

Write birthday cards to give to Jesus, praising Him for His incomparable gift—Himself in human flesh. The cards may be placed under the Christmas tree with the other gifts.

MONDAY—A Simple Activity

Throw a birthday party for Jesus. Enjoy a cake while talking about the difference between Jesus' birthday and a "normal" birthday—Jesus existed in heaven *before* His birth on earth.

TUESDAY—A Story Time

Read Luke 2:1-20 and light your third advent candle, the red one, representing Christ's blood.

WEDNESDAY—A Self-esteem Builder

Get out your family photo albums and go through the life history of each family member.

THURSDAY—A Family Worship Time

Light your fourth advent candle—white, representing Christ's holiness. Sing Christmas carols together and then see if you can recount the events in the first two chapters of Luke from memory. Assign someone with an open Bible to be a "prompter."

FRIDAY—Another Simple Activity

Create your own Christmas quiz for your family. Have two teams and ask questions such as: "In what city was Jesus born? Who was King when Jesus was born? What gifts did the wise men bring? Where did our family spend our first Christmas together? How many Christmases have Mom and Dad celebrated together?"

SATURDAY—A Special Event

Gather all of your Christmas cards together. Read them aloud, reminding the family who they were from. Pray for all the senders, thanking God for good friends. If you get a lot of cards, you may want to split this activity into several sessions. Hang the cards on a yarn or around a doorway so they are visible during the next three weeks.

ACTIVITY SUGGESTION: A great gift idea: Dad makes small cards that read, "The bearer is entitled to a day with Dad" and puts them in the kids' Christmas stockings.

WEEK 52

Living Value for the Week: THANKFULNESS
Special Celebration Days (optional): Fourth Week of Advent /
Christmas Day
Character: Jesus
Scripture: Matthew 2:1-23
Memory Verse: *"The virgin will be with child and will give birth to
a son, and will call him Immanuel."*—Isaiah 7:14b

Materials: thank-you notes
             small candles

Vision and passion: If you want to change your life or your world, you must have them in abundance. Vision sees how the world can be different. Passion makes it change.—Jerry MacGregor

SUNDAY—A Topic Introduction

On Christmas day, light the center advent candle, read Matthew 2:1-23 aloud, and sing "Joy to the World" before opening your gifts. Your children will long remember the traditions your family develops on holidays, so try to create a pattern to Christmas day that is fun, memorable, and relaxing.

MONDAY—A Simple Activity

Have everyone sit down together and write thank-you notes for the gifts they received. Doing this together makes it more fun—and ensures that the job will get done.

TUESDAY—A Story Time

Mom and Dad tell about: "My most wonderful Christmas ever."

WEDNESDAY—A Self-esteem Builder

End the year with a strength "bombardment." Have everyone sit in a circle with a chair in the middle. One person sits in that chair while the others bombard him or her with all the strengths they see in that person. The person being bombarded by encouraging comments must remain silent until everyone is finished speaking. After every one has had a turn, discuss how it feels to be so loved.

THURSDAY—A Family Worship Time

Ask everybody to go get their Christmas gifts and put them on the floor of your living room. Stand around them, holding hands, and ask, "Does God give us things to use only for ourselves? Does He expect us to guard them selfishly? To share them grudgingly? Does He allow us to have them so we'll feel good? Then WHY?" (Everything is to be used to do God's will, in a spirit of thankfulness.)

Announce that you're dedicating all of these things to God. Give everyone a candle. Have all take a turn lighting their candles and stating how they'll try to use their gifts (spiritual gifts, too!) for God's glory. (From *Devotions for Families that Can't Sit Still*)

FRIDAY—Another Simple Activity

Check an entire year's worth of memory verses. Anyone that can say five of them wins a trip to a pie-house for a fancy dessert! (Anyone who can't gets to go, too.)

SATURDAY—A Special Event

For a nice New Year's Eve together, get out the family scrapbook and update it for the year, then get out the family prayer notebook and update it. Spend some time praying together for the past year as well as the one to come.

Dr. MacGregor offers seminars on the subject
of discipling your children. For more information,
or if you have questions or a good discipleship
idea to pass along, write or call:

Dr. Jerry MacGregor
c/o Life-Trac Family Ministries
P.O. Box 755
Leavenworth, WA 98826
509) 548-4471

Christian Parenting
T O D A Y

☐ **YES,** please enter a subscription to *Christian Parenting Today* under my name at the address specified below.

☐ 1 year (6 issues) of *Christian Parenting Today* for only $16.97.

☐ 2 years (12 issues) of *Christian Parenting Today* for only $24.97.
Save $10.43!

NAME

ADDRESS

CITY   STATE   ZIP

For fast service with a credit card call
1-800-238-2221.

☐ Payment enclosed

☐ Bill me

Outside U.S. add $5.40 per
year in U.S. funds only
(GST included).

B2C21

Christian Parenting Today
P.O. Box 850
Sisters, OR 97759
1-800-238-2221